Late in the summer 1759, Québec, the capital of New France, was under siege. British Major General James Wolfe had the city surrounded and cut off from reinforcements in Montréal, Rear Admiral Charles Saunders was in firm control of the rivers surrounding the city as well as the supply routes into the region. The French population found itself low on food and ammunition to defend themselves, and suffering daily bombardment by the English. The walls of Québec were manned by militiamen and sailors taken from French ships lost or anchored above the city for their protection. *Lieutenant Général* Louis-Joseph de Montcalm-Gozon and his aide-de-camp Louis-Antoine de Bougainville commanded the French regulars outside the city, moving them in rapid deployments to counter the British advances.

Here the story is told by the citizens within the walls: an artillery captain, a prominent citizen, the emissary traveling between the British and the French commanders, and a Catholic nun working in the main hospital, treating the sick and wounded of both armies. Three of these works are offered in English for the first time, and all four are fully annotated. These journals and memoirs bring us inside the siege, allowing us to watch through their eyes as the fate of New France was determined.

Raised in the shadows of Fort Ticonderoga and Crown Point, Charles Mayhood, BSEd, is an independent researcher and historian focusing on the first-person journals and memoirs of those who witnessed the events from Albany, New York, to Quebec City during both the French & Indian and Revolutionary Wars.

Québec Under Siege

French Eye-Witness Accounts from the Campaign of 1759

Translated and annotated by Charles A. Mayhood

Helion & Company Limited

Helion & Company Limited
Unit 8 Amherst Business Centre
Budbrooke Road
Warwick
CV34 5WE
England
Tel. 01926 499619
Email: info@helion.co.uk
Website: www.helion.co.uk
Twitter: @helionbooks
Visit our blog at http://blog.helion.co.uk/

Published by Helion & Company 2019
Designed and typeset by Mach 3 Solutions Ltd (www.mach3solutions.co.uk)
Cover designed by Paul Hewitt, Battlefield Design (www.battlefield-design.co.uk)

ISBN 978-1-912866-73-1

British Library Cataloguing-in-Publication Data.
A catalogue record for this book is available from the British Library.

For details of other military history titles published by Helion & Company Limited, contact the above address, or visit our website: http://www.helion.co.uk

We always welcome receiving book proposals from prospective authors.

Dedicated to the memory of the original authors of these works, in recognition of their great sacrifice in service to New France, as well as to Jane M. Lape and John H.G. Pell in recognition of their lifelong commitment to preserving history through their work curating the Fort Ticonderoga Museum and Library.

Contents

List of Plates viii
List of Maps ix
Preface x
Introduction xii

1 François Jérôme Pierre de Foligné-Deschalonges 15
2 Jean-Claude Panet 71
3 Gilles-Armand Joannès 95
4 Marie-Joseph Legardeur de Repentigny, Sœur de la Visitation 104

Bibliography 121
Index 127

List of Plates

General view of Québec from Pointe de Lévy, 1759, etching by Richard Short, copied 1863, William Notman. (McCord Museum, I-6268.1) xiii

A View of the Bishop's House with the Ruins, Québec, 1759, etching by Richard Short, copied 1863 by William Notman. (McCord Museum, I-6410.1) 41

Plan of the ground floor of the *Hôpital Général* at Notre-Dame-des-Anges near Québec, Mademoiselle Saint-Ours, 6 October 1785 (Monastère des Augustines de l'Hôpital Général de Québec fonds. HG-A-23.15.12.1) 105

Plan of the first floor of the old and new building, 18th Century (Monastère des Augustines de l'Hôpital général de Québec fonds. HG-A-23.15.12.6) 106

List of Maps

1 Québec City. 18

2 Québec Theater of Operations. 27

3 Québec and Environs. 45

4 Battle of the Plains of Abraham, 13 September 1759. 60

Preface

Thanks are owed to the dedicated 19th and 20th century historians, as through their work we now have the privilege to visit the forts and fields where the fate of our continent was determined, and to walk in the shadow of those who battled for dominion over this vast wilderness. They collected items both rare and common, documents both grand and unimpressive, and they carefully tucked them away in vaults and museums so that future generations would have the opportunity to study them and develop an understanding of our shared past.

Unique among such collections are the first-person accounts of the events, major and minor, which transpired along this shared life-path, such as those presented in this book. These documents offer us the opportunity to join the authors in experiencing the events as they themselves watched them unfold. Without interpretation, without guessing, they tell us what stood out to them as having been important enough to note or to record in their journals and memoirs.

The four such works which form the substance of this book offer unique French points of view: a French naval officer assigned to command an artillery battery on the river's shore; a man who arrived from France at the age of 21 and rose to become a prominent leader in Québec society; a young officer in the regular French army, just 25 and already an engineer and respected leader serving his king and his country; and the daughter of a leading *Québécois* family dedicated to serving the poor and needy as an Augustinian Sister at the General Hospital.

These four works have long stood out as offering an alternative view to the better-known British perspective regarding the 1759 Siege of Québec, and each is taken from a previous 19th century publication. The Foligné and Panet journals, as well as the Joannès *mémoire*, have been translated here from the original French. The earlier editions appear to have kept closely to the original manuscripts, including the vagaries in spelling and grammar so very common in works from this time. Translating the Foligné was problematic in that it included a considerable number of typographical errors, so numerous that historian Aegidius Fauteux felt obliged to explain them while footnoting the journal in another work.

Several editorial choices have been made in an attempt to improve the reading experience. To reinforce the fact that these are French journals some words are left in their original form. Compound sentences are included, where they work, to maintain the feel of the time. Sentence structure, punctuation, and a very few words have been changed to make it more pleasurable to read. Names have been corrected when possible and biographical information included when it supplements the text. Spelling of location names has been made uniform throughout the book, their format adopted from period sources.

And through these works, *je me souviens.*

C.A. Mayhood

Introduction

By 1754 the French had claimed vast areas of North America: New France (Québec), along the Mississippi from *La Louisiane* to the Illinois country, and continued to spread westward along Lakes Ontario and Erie. Their settlements ranged from simple fortified trading posts, inhabited only by fur traders and their native contacts, to the cities of Montréal and Québec, with their walls and battlements for defense. The British, for their part, had settled the length of the eastern seacoast, spreading inland and establishing innumerable settlements; their principal cities included Williamsburg, Philadelphia, New York and Boston. Relations between the French and the British had long been problematic, with war having been declared off and on for most of the last 70 years. Each country sought to become the dominant European power with control over the lucrative trade routes worldwide.

The early 1700s had seen a rapid expansion in the British colonial population with a 1754 census showing 1,170,800 inhabitants. A French census that same year set the New France population at 55,009. The coastal area could no longer accommodate the British population and they began to migrate westward, encroaching on lands claimed by France. The situation became an open conflict in 1749 when French troops drove Pennsylvanian settlers from the upper Ohio River valley, insisting they retreat to the eastern side of the Appalachian mountains. Subsequent skirmishes and outright battles favored the French with repeated victories. The British, with ill-trained colonial militias and too few experienced officers, found themselves bested at Fort LeBœuf (1753), at Washington's battle at Great Meadows (1754) and at Fort Duquesne (1755).

Singular among these early battles was the successful British defense at Lake George in 1755, where Sir William Johnson and his Mohawk allies proved vital in defeating Baron Dieskau's forces and taking him prisoner. Indigenous populations became essential participants on both sides of the conflict, resulting in the North American experience of the wider Seven Years War becoming better known as the French and Indian War. By the official declaration of war in May 1756 the French in North America were already reeling. Even while successfully taking Fort William Henry (1757) and defending Carillon from a far superior British force (1758), they began to withhold their limited troops and materials for the protection of their lands in Canada, their battles planned and executed from a defensive point of view. The year 1758 saw the British fortunes turn, with the capture of the fortress at Louisbourg giving them unfettered control over the supply routes into Canada. New France thus faced their enemy on three fronts.

And so we reach 1759, the year of concern in this book. French North America was weakened due to waning support from France, self-interested and powerful profiteers in New France, and two successive failed harvests. Short of men and munitions to defend their cities and of food to feed their people, with the fast-approaching British forces, the French in North America teetered on the brink of extinction. In June, British forces under Brigadier Prideaux quickly captured Fort Oswego, then joined by Sir William Johnson and 1,000 Iroquois warriors they laid siege to Fort Niagara in mid-July, working their way eastward. The British fleet under Rear Admiral Saunders controlled the water routes and prevented any resupply from France. Major General Wolfe and his army were expected daily, advancing from Atlantic Canada, which had been under British control following the capture of Louisbourg. Major General Amherst and his troops were preparing to march north from Albany to challenge Forts Carillon and St Frédéric on his way to join Wolfe at Québec.

Clearly, after so many years of great successes over vast territories, the French in Québec were now under siege. With the war enveloping their homes and communities, our four French protagonists, whose writings are presented in this book, found themselves living each day in the hope that God or the King would save

General view of Québec from Pointe de Lévy, 1759, etching by Richard Short, copied 1863, William Notman. (McCord Museum, I-6268.1)

them. The insights we gain from reading their remarkable documents about the fighting and its consequences are detailed and sweeping as well as pungent and poignant.

I wish to thank five people who have provided essential insight and have willingly shared their specialized skills and research in forwarding my work: Julie Roy, historian and Manager of Reference Services for the Library and Archives of Canada, in Ottawa; Thomas Carr, Jr, emeritus professor of Modern Languages and Literature, University of Nebraska–Lincoln; Matthew Keagle, Curator of Collections at Fort Ticonderoga; Dr. David B. Knight, retired Canadian Professor of Political and Historical Geography; and William Raffle, historian, who has recently published the translated and annotated *Glories to Useless Heroism: The American Journals of Comte Maurès de Malartic, 1755–1760.*

1

François Jérôme Pierre de Foligné-Deschalonges

François Jérôme Pierre de Foligné-Deschalonges (also written as 'Foligny'), Chevalier de St Louis and French naval officer, was born on 29 September 1732 at Combourg, France, making him a young officer of 27 when this journal was written.

Foligné arrived in Québec while serving on the French merchant ship *Swinton* (*Schwinton*), under Captain Michel Guillon (or Gaillon), having sailed from the port of Nantes on 31 December 1758, and subsequently leaving Bordeaux on 10 January 1759.[1] The ship arrived in Québec on 18 May with a cargo of food and supplies for the troops.[2]

Foligné was soon assigned duties defending Québec. On 15 June, Governor-General Vaudreuil assigned him to work under François-Louis Poulin de Courval in the preparation of fire rafts. On 28 June, he was reassigned to command a battery in front of the city walls on the river shore, the position he held throughout the remaining journal.[3]

As the journal ends, Foligné was returning to France, where he would spend the greater part of 1760 fighting for his back pay and expense reimbursements from the siege, as well as seeking a brevet to *lieutenant de frégate* in the French Royal Navy.[4]

1 Charles Vianney Campeau, 'The Swinton', *Navires Venus en Nouvelle-France*, http://naviresnouvelle-france.net/vaisseau1700/html/page1759.html (accessed 4 September 2018).

2 Richard Couture, '1759: British expedition against Québec – preparations and arrival', *Kronoskaf Seven Years War Project*, http://www.kronoskaf.com/syw/index.php?title=1759_-_British_expedition_against_Qu%C3%A9bec_%E2%80%93_Preparations_and_Arrival (accessed 7 June 2019).

3 Archives Nationales D'Outre-Mer, Québec. Certificats accordés à Foligné Du Chalonge,' 1759, http://anom.archivesnationales.culture.gouv.fr/ark:/61561/bo755dxzz14z (accessed 4 September 2018).

4 Archives Nationales D'Outre-Mer, 'Foligné Du Chalonge (François Jérôme), commander of the *Schwinton*', http://anom.archivesnationales.culture.gouv.fr/ark:/61561/bo755ztvutwm (accessed 4 September 2018).

Foligné reappeared in North American history through his support of the Colonies during the Revolutionary War. In March 1777, Foligné captained one of Beaumarchais' secret committee ships, *Le Marquis de la Chalotais*, transporting clandestine war goods from France to the American Colonies.[5] Having completed his voyage in August, Foligné paid a visit to Benjamin Franklin, delivering letters and information to him from Peter Timothy and the South Carolina Congress.[6] After completing a subsequent successful mission in St Domingue, Foligné advanced in rank, in no small part thanks to a letter of recommendation sent by Franklin on 30 July 1779. His hopes for further advancement were stymied when, in 1780, Antoine de Sartine was replaced as French Secretary of State for the Navy by the Marquis de Castries, to whom Foligné was a complete unknown. He turned again to Franklin and asked for another letter of recommendation. History does not record whether Franklin ever supplied this second letter, but Foligné did make small advancements in 1782 and 1786, before retiring with his naval career ambitions unfulfilled in 1787.

François Jérôme Pierre de Foligné-Deschalonges died on 10 November 1804, after having served as a court officer in Nantes, as well as serving on the *Tribunal du Point d'Honneur* established by Louis XVI in an effort to end duels.[7]

5 K.N. Kellow, 'Le Marquis de la Chalotais', *American War of Independence – At Sea*, http://www.awiatsea.com/conn/Le%20Marquis%20de%20la%20Chalotais%20Ship%20Beaumarchais.html (accessed 4 September 2018).

6 US National Archives, Peter Timothy to Benjamin Franklin, 12 June 1777, *Founders Online*, https://founders.archives.gov/documents/Franklin/01-24-02-0122 (accessed 4 September 2018). Original source: William B. Willcox (ed.), *The Papers of Benjamin Franklin*, vol.24 (New Haven, CT: Yale University Press, 1984), pp.154–156.

7 Anon., 'Premier voyage à Saint-Domingue', https://www.decitre.fr/media/pdf/feuilletage/9/7/8/2/9/1/9/3/9782919339471.pdf (accessed 6 June 2019), footnote on p.12.

Journal of facts related to the Army of Québec, Capital in North America, During the campaign of the year 1759 by M. de Foligné[8]

Memorandum of the more memorable events during the siege of the city of *Québec*, capital of Canada, in North America, and facts related to our army made up of battalions of *La Sarre*, *Royal Roussillon*, *Guyenne*, *Béarn*, *Languedoc*, Colony troops and militia, making the number of 11 to 12 thousand men commanded in person by *Mr*[9] *le Marquis de Vaudreuil*, *Gouverneur Général* of all New France, *Mr le Marquis de Montcalm*, *Lieutenant Général* of His Majesty's Armies, the *Chevalier de Lévis*, *Maréchal de Camp* and *Mr De Senerzerque*, *Brigadier des Armées du Roi* commanding the Battalion *La Sarre*;[10] where *Mr De Foligné* serves, *Capitaine en Second* of the *Corvette Swinton*,[11] of Brest, working as the commander of the batteries in front of the ramparts on the river shore, having under his command 140 men, sailors, cannoneers, and servants to service 20 *cannons* of 18 and 12 [pounds] with two large *mortiers*.[12]

Description of the upper and lower city of *Québec*, Capital of North America

The city of *Québec* is located on a steep mountain, built like an amphitheater, having upper and lower towns in front of which passes the beautiful Rivière St Laurent, one of the largest in the world, its harbor is about 11 to 12 hundred *toises* in circumference bounded on the north by the small *Rivière St Charles*, which disappears into the countryside:[13] to the south and crossing in front of the city, the river can be 7 to 800 *toises* wide, to the east by the same river, forming the main channel of this beautiful river, here the harbor extends from NNE to SSW and can anchor ships from 28 fathoms to 14 with a very good bottom of muddy sand. The water is very clear and good to drink. To the west are the plains and

8 This translation has been completed using *Journal des Faits Arrivés à l'Armé de Québec, Capital dans l'Amérique Septentrional, Pendant la Campagne de l'Année 1759, par M. de Foligné* (Québec: The Community of Franciscan Sisters, 1901).

9 Foligné's chosen shorthand for 'Monsieur' in his journal.

10 *Maréchal de Camp* is the French rank indicating a brigade command under the general and the lieutenant general.

11 A *corvette* is the smallest of the warships, usually flat-decked and having a single tier of guns. *Le Swinton* (*Schwinton*), Michel Guillon (or Gaillon), *capitaine*. *Proprio*: Bassemaison et Cameret, de Brest. *Armateur*: Féger *frères* et Corbun. Campeau, *Navires Venus en Nouvelle-France*.

12 Mortars.

13 Derived from the ancient French *teise*, a *toise* is an area of measurement which includes length, area, and volume which was approximately 3.8 square meters. For distance measurements one *toise* would have been roughly equivalent to two meters.

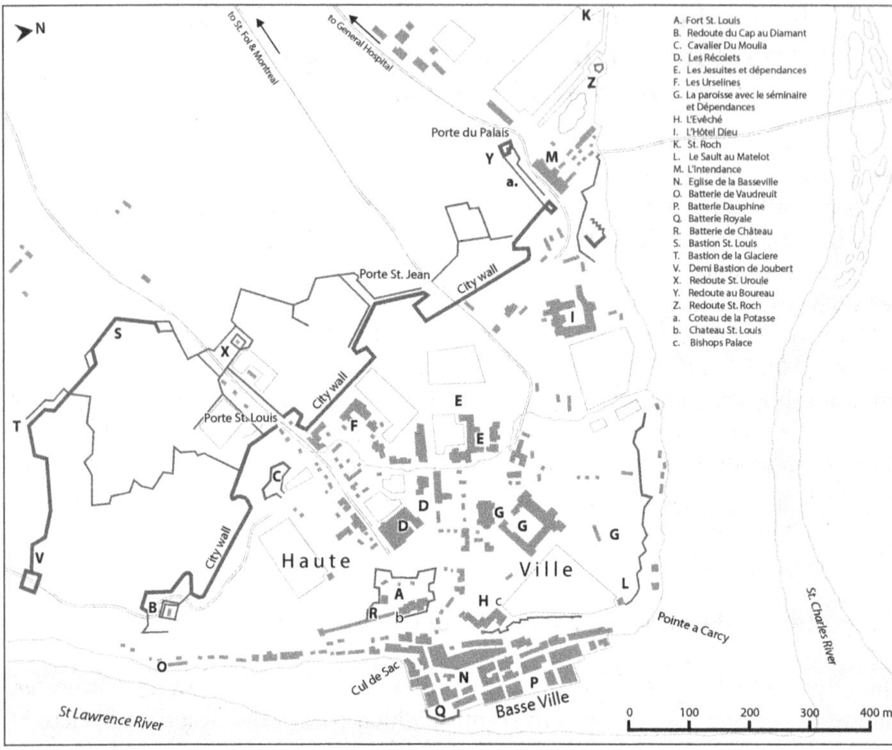

Map 1 Québec City.

the Royal Road that leads to the city of *Montréal*, enclosed with a very weak wall from the SSW to NNW, elevated from 25 to 30 *pieds* with various ditches but no advanced works,[14] this whole rampart is lined with 52 guns, from 12 to 2 pound balls, unbreachable by assault as all the flanks and defiles are covered should the enemy attempt to climb the walls.[15]

Québec has three gates on the water side, without drawbridges, including one in the SSW which is called *Porte St Louis*, which leads to the *Côte d'Abraham*, and Samos; the second is called *Porte St Jean*, which leads to the road to *St Foi* parish, a league and a half from *Québec*. The third gate is called the *Porte du Palais*, leading into the suburbs and *St Roche*. This path goes straight to the General Hospital, founded by *Mr de Saint-Vallier*, second bishop of *Québec*, to serve thirty to forty indigents; since the war this hospital has cared for the sick of the regular troops, the Sisters of Mercy of Jesus, under the rule of St Augustine, serve this hospital,

14 From Old French *pié*, a unit of measure equal to 32.5 cm.

15 A defile is a narrow passage designed to force troops into a tight column or front.

they are well known for their charity work for the poor. This same gate also leads to the road for the parishes of *Beauport* and *Charlesbourg*, two leagues from the city. The northern boundary is very steep with palisades six feet high defended by three small batteries of 8 guns of 18 and 12 pounds.[16]

The ramparts facing the river, which defend the harbor, are mounted from NNE to SSE with 42 guns, of 24, 18, and 12 pounds, with six large iron *mortiers* and one of bronze;[17] all this battery is *en barbette*, supported by a poor stone wall.[18]

From SSE to SSW this section of the ramparts is lined with palisades that join the end of the SSW wall, defended by two different batteries of 16 guns of 24, 18, 12, and 8 pounds, with two *mortiers*.

The lower city, where the business district stands, is protected by four different batteries that cover the harbor, equipped with 36-, 24-, 18-, 12-, and 8-pound guns; these batteries are called *Batterie St Charles*, the *Batterie Dauphine*, *Batterie Royale*, and *Batterie de la Construction*.

The *Palais de l'Intendant*,[19] which lies outside the city to the WNW, beside the *Rivière St Charles*, where there is a wharf defended by several guns and several double palisades, on the road to *St Roche*. On the road between the upper and lower towns there are two batteries, *en barbette*, of four cannons which defend the road. Such were the forces of the capital of New France when the whole colony was waiting for news from Europe, each day expecting to find themselves blockaded, etc. etc.

The 12th of May – At eight PM, came *Mr Bougainville*,[20] *Colonel*, *Chevalier de St Louis*,[21] carrying the court packets, with no further news of the frigate *Chézine*, on which he had crossed.[22] His arrival caused so much joy that news of his arrival

16 *Pallisade*: a closely-set line of long wooden stakes, usually sharpened to a point on the exposed end, driven into the ground as a defense.

17 The manuscript uses '*mortiers de fer et de fonte*', at this time indicating iron and a bronze mortars. In later usage '*de fonte*' usually refers to cast iron. Matthew Keagle, Curator, Fort Ticonderoga Museum, e-mail, 28 July 2018.

18 *En barbette* indicates a fortification using a platform or a mound of earth to raise guns so that they can fire over a wall or parapet.

19 The *Intendant* was the head of the civil administration in New France, who oversaw justice, finance and commerce, policing, currency, militia, and presided over the Sovereign Council.

20 Louis-Antoine, Comte de Bougainville (1729–1811) *Capitaine* and aide-de-camp to the Marquis de Montcalm in 1756, participant in the capture of Oswego and Fort William Henry, and the 1758 defense of Carillon. Étienne Taillemite, 'Bougainville, Louis-Antoine de, Comte de Bougainville,' in *Dictionary of Canadian Biography*, vol.5 (Toronto: University of Toronto/Université Laval, 2003–).

21 The creation of the Royal and Military Order of St Louis was signed by Louis XIV on 5 April 1693. The order was to consist of eight Grand Crosses, 28 Commanders, and the number of Knights His Majesty thought fit to admit. Laurent Lamole, 'L'Ordre royale et militaire de Saint-Louis,' *Les Ordres de Chevalerie*, http://lorl.free.fr/stlouis.htm (accessed 25 July 2018).

22 Letters and other communications carried from the Court of Louis XV, including orders and instructions for Governor-General Vaudreuil and his army.

was spread throughout the city, this news being all the more interesting in that it brought word of a fleet, expected shortly, of seventeen ships coming from *Bourdeaux* and loaded with war goods and provisions, under the escort of the frigate *Macheault*,[23] commanded by *Mr Kanon, Lieutenant de frégatte*.[24] No joy was ever more general, it lifted the hearts of all the people who, during the difficult winter, had been reduced to a quarter of bread and a half-*livre* of horse meat. That was the situation of the Canadian people when *Mr Bougainville* arrived, who after having landed, left in the night for *Montréal* where our generals were. The *Général*[25] and *Mr le Marquis de Montcalm*[26] had not yet received the court packets, which gave them reconnaissance of the English armaments for the conquest of our colony and that the enemy fleet would soon appear on the river, which knowing this, the *Marquis de Montcalm* left *Montréal* where he had been since March, to organize our army for the *Carillon* campaign.[27]

The 16th of May – The *Marquis de Montcalm* with *Mr le Chevalier de Lévis*[28] arrived to cheers from all the people of the city of *Québec*, refusing to receive any visitors being only interested in seeing the instructions they had received from the court.

The 17th of May – Our generals inspected the places where they thought the enemy might try to make their landing, to note the advantages of the ground. They saw the difficulties that they would have in defending it, a distance of two leagues being considerable and with few men, it was this section that our generals inspected, from the *Rivière St Charles* to *Sault Montmorency*;[29] to cover the city, they planned to fortify the land they came to review. Before reaching the city, our

23 *Marchault* (*Machault*): 500–550 ton, as a civilian vessel Jacques Kanon (Canon), *capitaine*. *Proprio*: Pierre Desclaux & *Fils aîné*. Campeau, *Navires Venus en Nouvelle-France*.

24 Jaçques Kanon, privateer and naval officer. His ship was one of only three French ships to reach Québec in 1759. James S. Pritchard, 'Kanon, Jacques,' in *Dictionary of Canadian Biography*, vol.3 (Toronto: University of Toronto/Université Laval, 2003–).

25 Throughout the journal Foligné uses 'the General' to refer to Gouverneur-Général Pierre de Rigaud, Marquis de Vaudreuil-Cavagnial.

26 Louis-Joseph de Montcalm-Gozon, Marquis de Montcalm de Saint-Veran (1712–1759) Commander of French forces in North America during the Seven Years War, a French nobleman who joined the army in 1721 and served with distinction during the Polish and Austrian Wars of Succession. W.J. Eccles, 'Montcalm, Louis-Joseph, Marquis de Montcalm,' in *Dictionary of Canadian Biography*, vol.3 (Toronto: University of Toronto/Université Laval, 2003–).

27 Carillon was the southernmost French position in 1759, also known as Ticonderoga by the British.

28 François-Gaston de Lévis, Duc de Lévis (1719–1787) Commonly called the *Chevalier de Lévis*, Montcalm's second in command in New France, having previously served with him during the Polish and Austrian Wars of Succession. (Foligné uses 'Lévy'.) W.J. Eccles, 'Lévis, François de, Duc de Lévis,' in *Dictionary of Canadian Biography*, vol.4 (Toronto: University of Toronto/Université Laval, 2003–).

29 Montmorency Falls, located 12 km from Québec City, between the parishes of Beauport and Boischatel. Here the Montmorency River drops 83 m to the Rivière St Laurent, at the western end of the Isle d'Orléans.

generals were met by a courier sent by *Mr Aubert,*[30] posted at *St Barnabe*, and from the courier learning the first division of 15 enemy vessels were near the channel at *Bic*, 60 leagues from *Québec*.[31] This first news of the arrival of the enemy on our river was confirmed by one of our ships coming from *Brest*, which had no knowledge of our *Bordeaux* fleet. The ship had started to travel with our vessels, which he did for about a day. It is only when they arrived at *Isle aux Coudres* that the inhabitants told him *Mr Kanon*'s fleet had arrived safely,[32] with the exception of three ships of the fleet for which the captain of this last vessel did not wait, rather he detached one of his officers to our generals to make his report, at which the *Marquis de Montcalm* sent orders to the battalions of the *Sarre*, *Royal Roussillon*, *La Reine*, *Languedoc*, *Guyenne*, and *Béarn*, who were still in their various quarters, to prepare with all diligence, that as soon as they arrived he would act. On the 24th, 26th, 27th, and 28th our troops arrived at the General Hospital on the *Rivière St Charles*, 3/4 of a league from *Québec*. On the 21st two of our frigates from *Brest* entered *Québec* harbor, loaded with war goods, and a fleet from *Rochefort* laden with flour and powder.

On the evening of the 23rd the *Marquis de Vaudreuil*,[33] Governor-General [of New France], arrived. The next day he detached several officers to dispatch his orders; *Mr de St Vincent Capitaine* and *Chevalier de St Louis*,[34] with two *lieutenants*, left for the *Isle d'Orléans* where he had to force the inhabitants to evacuate north with all their households.[35] *Mr de Léry*,[36] *Capitaine*, with some junior officers, departed for the south coast to compel the inhabitants from the *Camouraskas* to

30 Ignace-Philippe Aubert de Gaspé (1714–1787) Officer in the colonial regular troops; promoted *capitaine* 1756, participated at taking of Fort William Henry and the defense of Carillon. Jacques Castonguay, 'Aubert de Gaspé, Ignace-Philippe,' in *Dictionary of Canadian Biography*, vol.4 (Toronto: University of Toronto/Université Laval, 2003–).

31 Isle du Bic is located north-east of Québec City on the southern shore of the Rivière St Laurent and offered a naturally protected anchorage. Foligné uses the spelling 'Bique'.

32 Hazel Island, named for the abundant nut trees on the island. North-east of the Isle d'Orléans near the Baie St Paul.

33 Pierre de Rigaud de Vaudreuil de Cavagnial (1698–1778) Noble, officer of colonial regulars, governor of Montréal, and last Governor-General of New France. W.J. Eccles, 'Rigaud de Vaudreuil de Cavagnial, Pierre de, Marquis de Vaudreuil,' in *Dictionary of Canadian Biography*, vol.4 (Toronto: University of Toronto/Université Laval, 2003-).

34 Henri Albert de St. Vincent, Sieur de Narcy (1697–1762) '(3) … son of a prominent member of the Canadian noblesse, was ensign in 1727, lieutenant in 1742, and captain in 1749. He was at Lorette in 1730, was sent with a convoy to Machinac in 1747, and signed the capitulation of Quebec (1759).' Reuben Gold Thwaites (ed.), 'The French regime in Wisconsin – II 1727–1748,' in *Collections of the State Historical Society of Wisconsin*, vol.17 (Madison, WI: published by the Society, 1906), footnote on p.428.

35 Isle d'Orléans is an island in the Rivière St Laurent 5 km east of Québec City, a focal point for early colonization in New France.

36 Gaspard-Joseph Chaussegros de Léry (1721–1797) Military engineer in New France during the Seven Years War, sometimes referred to as Joseph-Gaspard to differentiate from his father of the same name and

move above the *Sault de la Chaudière*, two leagues to the south of the city, but the latter preferred to disappear into the depths of the woods despite the General's orders. This first precaution taken, *Mr le Général* detached other officers carrying his orders to all places of government – orders to *capitaines* of parishes to gather whomever would be able to bear arms, and to leave immediately to come and camp with our regular troops, ordered to arrive daily, all young and old; everyone is finding the strength to carry arms, and be with the party here. I must praise the Canadians, that never were orders received with more joy and executed with more accuracy. So the *Marquis de Montcalm* passed the beginning of June, at the head of an army of 11 to 12 thousand men, all happy to do their duty well.

The *Marquis de Montcalm*, seeing the positive disposition of his army, wanted to take advantage of it to put everyone to work; accordingly he ordered *Mr de Pontleroy*, chief engineer, to mark out the field works where our generals thought the battlefield would be.[37]

The 28th of May – We started to throw up floating bridges on the *Rivière St Charles* for easier communication between the city and the different posts, we began by raising redoubts at both ends for the defense of the bridge,[38] and a parapet running from *St Roche* along the *Rivière St Charles* over a quarter league, to above the General Hospital, at the end of which one finds the last bridge connecting opposite the English ground.

The 2nd of June – Fresh winds from the East North East, the weather rainy. Some inhabitants of *Baie St Paul* arrived, who reported that the 15 English vessels which had been seen at *Bic* had arrived in the harbor of *Isle aux Coudres* on the 23rd of last month, upon which our generals decided to hold a council of war, to which our naval officers were called; it was decided by this first council that we would sink eight of our ships in the channel, but first we wanted to sound it. *Mr Pelegrin, lieutenant* of the gate nearest to the river, received orders accordingly;[39] but on

career. (Foligné uses 'Lerry'.) F.J. Thorpe, 'Chaussegros de Léry, Gaspard-Joseph (1721–97)', in *Dictionary of Canadian Biography*, vol.4 (Toronto: University of Toronto/Université Laval, 2003–).

37 Nicolas Sarrebource de Pontleroy (1717–1802) Nobleman, military engineer beginning in 1736. Fought in the Austrian War of Succession, assigned to the reconstruction of Louisbourg and oversaw the preparations for the 1758 defense of Carillon (Foligné uses 'de Pontle Roy'). F.J. Thorpe, 'Sarrebource de Pontleroy, Nicolas,' in *Dictionary of Canadian Biography*, vol.5 (Toronto: University of Toronto/ Université Laval, 2003–).

38 A redoubt is an exterior defensive enclosure, most often of earthen construction, built to strengthen a position or to offer cover to advanced posts.

39 Gabriel Pellegrin (Pelegrin) (1713–1788) mariner and naval officer, 1751 accepted post as harbor master at Québec. Respected by Montcalm, assisted in defensive planning along the Rivière St Laurent, his suggestions forwarded but not acted upon. See source for considerable detail of event cited in the journal. James S. Pritchard, 'Pellegrin, Gabriel', in *Dictionary of Canadian Biography*, vol.4 (Toronto: University of Toronto/Université Laval, 2003–).

his return he reports finding it impossible to carry out what had been decided at the war council, but a report from our Canadian *marins* states that it has been felt that this crossing alone was a hindrance to an enemy's efforts,[40] so they are embarrassed to have waited to see the enemy before knowing the opposite is true, to have misled the court, to have exposed the King's army and a whole colony with risks, for not having bothered to probe. If they had acted like faithful subjects, they would have identified thousands of *toises* besides the two hundred and fifty they said they had, and would have taken other steps to secure their capital.

The 3rd of June – The *Chevalier Niverville*,[41] head of the Colony troops, who had been sent with 30 French and about as many Abenaki savages to scout the enemy at *Isle aux Coudres*, hoping to capture some prisoners, arrived without having dared to land on the island, the savages not wanting to take the risk. *Mr Desrivières* returned to *Québec* when *Mr de Niverville* agreed.[42] That same day *Mr de Repentigny*,[43] *capitaine* of Colony troops, *Chevalier de St Louis*, received orders to take a detachment of five hundred men to observe and guard the post of *St Joachim* parish, ten leagues north of *Québec*. *Mr de Courtemanche*, *capitaine* of Colony troops, with about a thousand men, all French and savages, was sent to build a camp north-east of *Isle d'Orléans*, three leagues from the city.[44] The

40 *Compagnies franches de la Marine*: independent companies under the Ministry of the Marine, formed in 1622 to protect French interests along the sea and outside its European boundaries, served in ports, on warships, and starting in 1683 as garrison troops in North America. By 1755 the majority of officers were Canadian-born, and until that year they were the only French regular infantry troops in Canada. Andrew Gallup and Donald F. Schaffer, *La Marine: The French Colonial Soldier in Canada, 1745–1761* (Bowie, MD: Heritage Books, 1992).

41 Joseph-Claude Boucher de Niverville (1715–1804) Army and militia officer as well as western explorer and Indian department official in New France. Participated at the taking of Fort William Henry and the defense of Carillon. Pierre Dufour, 'Boucher de Niverville, Joseph', in *Dictionary of Canadian Biography*, vol.5 (Toronto: University of Toronto/Université Laval, 2003–).

42 Eustache Trottier Desrivières (Foligné uses 'Deriviere') Merchant [translated from French] '(81) These were seven Canadians, led by M. Trottier Desrivières, a trader recently returned from a trip to France. It was M. Niverville who sent them off, after realizing the failure of his expedition. (cf. *Journal de Foligné*, p.168, et *Journal de Malartic*, p.239)': Anon., *Journal du Siège de Québec du 10 Mai au 18 Septembre 1759* (ed. Aegidius Fauteux) (Québec: Bibliothécaire de Saint-Sulpice, 1922), http://collections.banq.qc.ca/bitstream/52327/2022303/1/133074.pdf (accessed 2 September 2018), p.77.

43 Louis Legardeur de Repentigny (1721–1786) Began his military service at the age of 13 and was promoted to *enseigne* in 1748, *lieutenant* in 1751 and *capitaine* in 1759, participant in the battles of Fort William Henry (1757) and Carillon (1758). In the Québec campaign he commanded the army reserve. Étienne Taillemite, 'Legardeur de Repentigny, Louis,' in *Dictionary of Canadian Biography*, vol.4 (Toronto: University of Toronto/Université Laval, 2003–).

44 Jacques-François le Gardeur de Courtemanche (Foligné uses 'Courtemange') [translated from French] '(96) Jacques-François LeGardeur de Courtemanche, born in 1711, the son of Charles LeGardeur, Sieur de Croisille, and of Marie-Anne Robineau. Second ensign in 1736, first ensign in 1743, lieutenant in 1748, he was made captain in 1756 and a Chevalier de St. Louis on June 24, 1760. …' Anon., *Journal du Siège de Québec*, p.79.

Marquis de Montcalm, together with the *Chevalier de Lévis*, was busy progressing the work along the river from *Sault Montmorency* to the entrance to the *Rivière St Charles*: never did works rise more quickly, than those our generals had the satisfaction of seeing themselves, soon ready to receive the enemy in their descent; nothing could be more beautiful than these entrenchments, defended at intervals by good redoubts mounted with many pieces of cannon, two armed vessels at the entrance to the small river having ten cannons, a natural chain, in other words, making it impossible to force entry past our waiting batteries from the docks.

The 4th of June – The *Marquis de Montcalm* made an address in which he exhorted all those who are or would be useless in the service of our army, or who would serve in fear, to withdraw to the areas of *Trois Rivières* or *Montréal*. This same day, between six to seven o'clock in the evening, *Mr Desrivières* arrived with three prisoners – all three marine guards – including the youngest, who happens to be the grandson of the second admiral.

The 5th of June – *Mr de Repentigny* dispatched a courier notifying the generals that the first division of enemy ships, after easily making the traverse, were anchored near the end of *Isle d'Orléans*. This same day a letter from *Mr Aubert* arrived, announcing a second division of about 20 ships that appeared at *Bic* on the evening of the 2nd, which had been announced the third of the month by signal fires, which announced each arrival of enemy vessels at the *Isle du Bic*. This same day *Mr de Courtemanche*, watching the shores of *Isle d'Orléans*, reported the situation of the enemy who were anchored at half a cannon's shot across from his camp, and that the *Chevalier Mercier* was instructed to build a battery and that, having been completed, he asked for 4 guns, which he received in the night and he immediately established the battery and the next day found themselves able to fire and force the enemy to retreat.[45]

The 6th of June – *Monseigneur*, the bishop, after the request from the General, at nine a.m. sent for the Reverend Father Commissioner to whom he assigned five of his religious, for the chaplaincy of our army, who after receiving their faculties from His Excellency were distributed in different posts. *Père Gabriel*, by the request of *Mr de Montcalm* and *Mr de Senezergues*[46] with whom he had the honor

45 François-Marc-Antoine le Mercier (1722–1798) Native of Québec, artillery officer. In very Catholic Canada it is notable that he was not baptized until three days after his wedding in 1757, aged 35. Participant in the Polish War of Succession, arrived in Canada as a cadet of the colonial troops in 1740. Studied engineering and artillery. Jean Pariseau, 'Le Mercier, François-Marc-Antoine,' in *Dictionary of Canadian Biography*, vol.4 (Toronto: University of Toronto/Université Laval, 2003–).

46 Étienne-Guillaume de Senezergues de la Rodde (1709–1759) Officer in the French regiment La Sarre, entering military service at the age of 14. Commissioned *enseigne* in 1726, *lieutenant* in 1727, *capitaine* in 1734. Participated in both the Polish and Austrian Wars of Succession. Sent to America in 1756 as

of serving in three previous campaigns, was assigned to the regular troops, and accordingly he received authorization specific for *Mr de Senere*'s brigade composed of the five battalions.

The 7th of June – At 2 in the afternoon, in front of the whole city, we launched a floating battery, an invention of *Mr Duclos*, Captain of the frigate *La Chézine*.[47] His best invention, the battery will mount twelve guns, will be made in the image of a turtle, built with a flat, bare bottom usable at low tide, drawing 3 or 4 feet of water, this war machine was no sooner armed than she was taken to the construction docks to be seen from the *Château* by our generals.[48] The General has ordered that its inventor is to stand at the *Beauport* battery, to defend the entrance to the *Sault Montmorency* channel.

From the 7th to the 18th we were preparing to receive the enemy. A courier arrived at 2 p.m., coming from *Mr Aubert*'s post, and informed our generals of the arrival of the large fleet, appearing to be 130 in number, and so many sails arrived at *Bic* on the 16th that the fires lit to announce them were continuous. In the field, *Mr de Vaudreuil* immediately gave orders to all the captains of the King's frigates and merchant ships to sail their vessels at high water, going 15 leagues above *Québec* on the *Richelieu* [River], and as soon as they arrived at their destination to quickly return their officers and sailors, being sure to leave enough of their seamen to maneuver and guard their ships.

On the 21st the General's orders were executed to the letter, the nice ENE winds freshening, all the ships of our small fleet set sail and easily relocated higher on the *Richelieu*, several ships went up to *Montréal.*

On the *22nd* the eight to nine hundred officers and sailors of the vessels were back. The *Chevalier Mercier, commandant* of the artillery, received orders from the *Général* to employ everyone on the different batteries of both the city and the entrenchments, as he knows best about servicing cannon: the zeal of our sailors deserves the praise of our army, as well as the satisfaction of being particularly

a *lieutenant colonel*, leading the second battalion of his regiment. Participant at Oswego, Fort William Henry and the defense of Carillon. Promoted to *brigadier* in 1759, becoming Montcalm's second in command at Québec after de Lévis left for Montréal. (Foligné uses 'Senerzerque' and 'Senere'.) W.J. Eccles, 'Senezergues de la Rodde, Étienne-Guillaume de,' in *Dictionary of Canadian Biography*, vol.3 (Toronto: University of Toronto/Université Laval, 2003–).

47 Pierre-Nicolas Guyot (Guyon), *dit* Duclos (1722–1794), *Capitaine* of *La Chézine*, 400–430 tons, out of Nantes 31 December 1758. *Proprio*: Pierre Desclaux. The ship was captured by the British on 20 December 1759. (Foligné uses 'Dullos'.) Campeau, *Navires Venus en Nouvelle-France*.

48 *Château* St Louis, official residence of the Governor-General of New France.

honored with the protection of our generals, who could not help admiring the courage of our sailors.

The 23rd of June – The English fleet made the crossing and they joined the first divisions under *Isle d'Orléans*. This vast fleet is made up of 29 large ships of which three have three decks, 12 frigates and corvettes, 2 *galliotes à bombes*,[49] 80 transport ships, and 50 to 60 small boats or *goélettes*,[50] anchored from the tip of *Pointe de Lévy* to *Isle Madame* in two lines;[51] the next day they landed about 30 flat *bâteaux* from their ships, each capable of carrying 80 to 100 men, with more than 80 barges to be used for their landing.[52]

The 26th of June – At the morning tide a ship accompanied by two frigates appeared in the basin under their topsail, in the traverse from the church of *Pointe de Lévy*, making observations and swaggering; several batteries of the lower village fired cannons uselessly, the ships being out of range.

The 27th of June – The *Marquis de Montcalm* gave orders to raise the camp behind the General Hospital, and to occupy the ground along the entrenchments. The *Chevalier de Lévis*, with some of the colony's troops, *Montréal* militia and the regiment of *Royal Roussillon* making up 4 to 5 thousand men, are to occupy the head from the *Sault* to the *Beauport* church, where the *Guyenne* regiment will camp, forming a line up to the three battalions of *Béarn*, *Languedoc* and *La Sarre*, occupying the center of the army, where *Mr de Vaudreuil* and the *Marquis de Montcalm* were to camp, the *Trois Rivières* and *Montréal* battalions to extend from *La Sarre* battalion to the *Canardière*, *Mr de Bougainville* to command this last camp.[53] This same day, the *Marquis de Vaudreuil* having given orders to launch four fireships into *Québec* harbor, they set sail at the evening tide from the cove at *Cap Rouge*, and at a quarter to eight they regrouped in the harbor before the city:[54] Command of the fireships must be given to a brave and cautious man, who would volunteer

49 *Galliotes à bombes*: bomb ketches armed with a mortar mounted near the bow. Their shells were called bombs or carcasses, a type of incendiary shell filled with a highly flammable fluid.

50 *Goélettes*: schooners.

51 *Isle Madame* – Below the NE end of the Isle d'Orléans, in the Rivière St Laurent.

52 *Bâteau* (pl. *bâteaux*): in North America the *bâteau* was the work-horse boat of the period. *Bâteaux* were usually 25 to 35 feet long, with flat bottoms and flaring sides, with bows and sterns which angled straight up from the water line. This shape maximized the interior space and allowed travel in the sometimes shallow waters of the region. They were propelled by oars or poles, steered by a stern sweep. They were commonly built of pine planks with oak frames.

53 *The Canardière*: the area above the St Charles River, NW of Québec City, traversed by the roads to Charlesbourg and Beauport.

54 *Cap Rouge*: on the north shore of the Rivière St Laurent, between St Augustin and St Foi, south of Québec City.

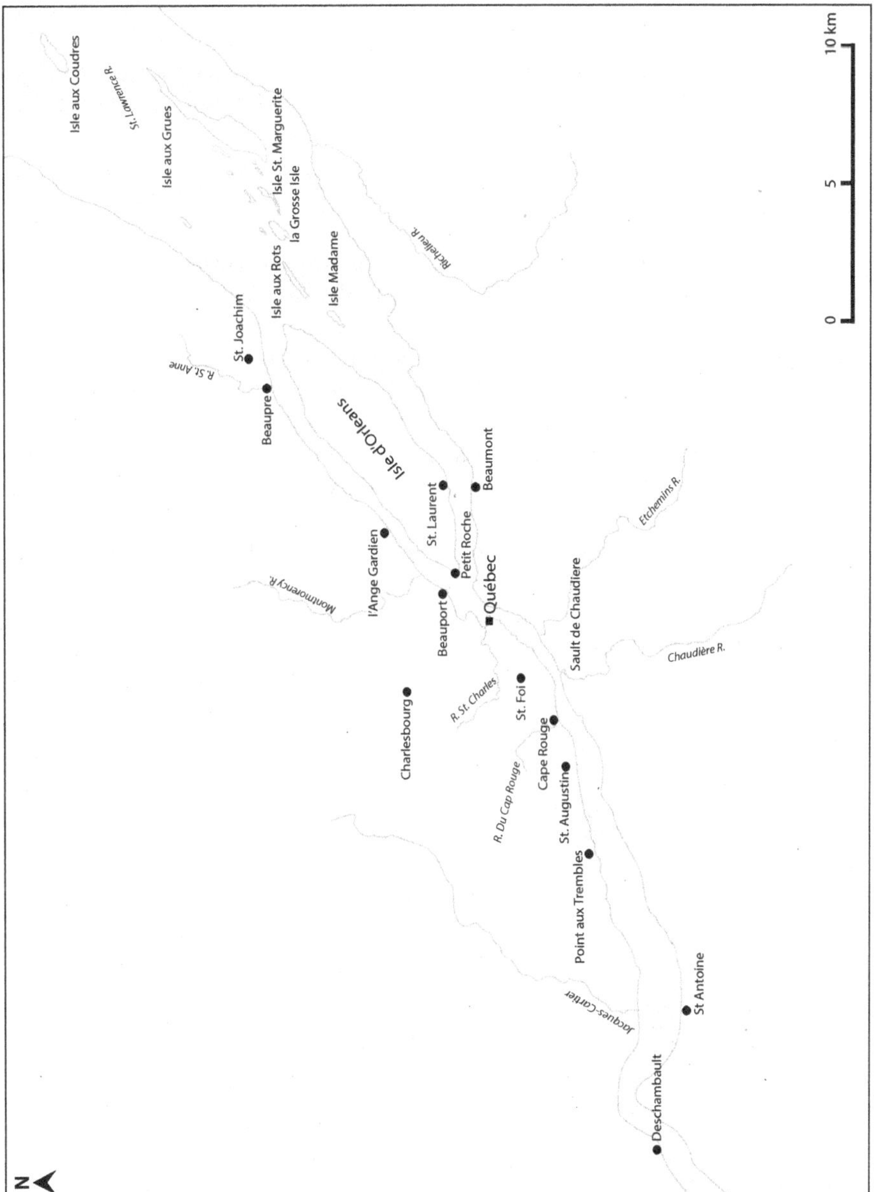

Map 2 Québec Theater of Operations.

to undertake such a dangerous mission: *Sieur Delouche*,[55] *Capitaine* commanding the vessel *l'Américain*,[56] a young man at the flower of his age, pushed by the feelings that inspire us – the love of country and glory – was persuaded to try, without thinking about the dangers which demand unequaled bravery and prudence, thought to ask for the command of the eight fireships, which the *Général* granted happily; he [Delouche] had under his command *Messrs Grandmont, Deschamps, Berthelot, Sabourin, de Loumeau, Marchand*, and *Dubois de la Miltière*;[57] all felt it right that command went to *Sieur Delouche*, who impressed the importance of success on the sailors of the expedition.

The 28th of June – The *Général* ordered *Sieur Delouche* to arrange everything for the fireship expedition, in order to leave in the night. *M. Delouche* set nine to ten o'clock as the best time, with fresh SW winds. He had hardly sailed a cannon's shot away from the city when fear and panic, no doubt, seized the heart of *Sr Delouche*, which led him to set fire to his fireship when the English fleet was still more than a league and a half distant. The others, following his example, did the same, with the exception of *Mr Dubois de la Miltière*, a brave officer who, despite the bad actions of his companions, continued on his way for another half an hour or so, to the north of *Pointe de Lévy* where he was forced to touch off his devices, having two fireships in front and behind, which he could not avoid due to the great current that carried them: in the end he found himself so engaged that he did not have the time to save himself in his *chaloupe*, or it had already embarked his crew who abandoned him.[58] Unable to save himself, the brave officer perished in the flames with his captain, the second and one of his sailors; all the other officers and seamen of the fireships escaped without injury and were ashamed to

55 François Delouche (de Louches) de St-Denis (1724–?), Québec-born *Capitaine* of *L'Américain*, for which see 56; Anon., 'Huppe/Mailhot/Royals', *Rootsweb*, https://wc.rootsweb.com/cgi-bin/igm.cgi?op=GET&db=huppe1&id=I211128 (accessed 26 July 2018).

56 *L'Américain*, 400–450 tons out of Bordeaux, *Proprio* & *Armateur*: La Malétie et La Tuilière. Campeau, *Navires Venus en Nouvelle-France*.

57 Grandmont (Jean Gramont), commanding the fireship *l'Angélique* which he had brought from Bordeaux. 450–500 tons, *Proprio*: La Malétie et La Tuilière. (Foligné uses 'Grand Mont.') *Leseau/Descamps*: 'The only difference is that he [journal author] wrote Leseau where we [editors] had to write Descamps. The spelling of Foligné's journal is bad enough that a copyist might easily read Leseau instead of Descamps.' … 'We gladly give the benefit of the doubt to the anonymous author of the *Journal du Siège de Québec*, who almost never departs from the true spelling in proper names.' Possibly Pierre Roger Deschamps, master sailor, mentioned by Tanguay (III, 366). Berthelot, commanding the fireship *Jaloux Sabourin*, Lieutenant on *Atalante*, Jean Vauquelain Capt., *Proprio*: Le Roi. De Loumeau, merchant officer commanding the *goélette Mercier* had used on the 23rd. (Foligné uses 'Lourmeau'.) Marchand, *Capitaine* of *La Toison d'Or* from Bordeaux, but that ship was wrecked and burned on 8 June. No indication of the vessel in this attack. Pierre-Honoré Dubois de la Miltière, he has two brothers serving in the Languedoc Regiment here, commanding the fireship *l'Ambassadeur*, *Proprio*: DuBois de la Miltière. (Foligné uses 'Multiere'.) Anon., *Journal du Siège de Québec*, endnote 168, p.89. Campeau, *Navires Venus en Nouvelle-France*.

58 A *chaloupe* is a launch or a longboat.

see their ships burn in the sight of enemy ships without spreading the fire. Such an action, without doubt, delighted the English. Our generals, who had relocated to the church in *Beauport* wanting to observe *Sieur Delouche*'s maneuver, had just witnessed the failure and regretted having refused the command to *Mr Courval*, a brave and careful man, having the interest of the colony where he was born at heart, who with the sailors would have conducted a more glorious action for the nation;[59] Never were whispers more general among the people, nor had effrontery forced itself to a higher degree than on the part of *Sieur Delouche*, who, instead of hiding, appeared the next day at the *Château* certain of the favor which the General would show him, the latter, after a slight reprimand, received him indeed, as *Sieur Delouche* had imagined, much to the regret of the entire colony and especially of our sailors who would require that these remaining men re-embarked in a fire-ship, in order to repair their honor and that of the corps; but *Sieur Delouche*, who had set out to test his courage, avoided the idea. It is glorious for *Sieur Sabourin*, lieutenant on the frigate *l'Atalante*,[60] commanding a fireship, to have remained in the harbor during the previous unfortunate event, having noticed at the departure the discord which had sown among our fireship captains. *Sieur Sabourin* wanting to set aside all reproaches, embarked with part of his volunteer force on another fireship, on board which he worked to persuade the captain to set the fire only when they were within the [British] fleet. *Sr Sabourin*'s plan exposed this captain to too much danger, he preferred to imitate *Sieur Delouche* in his actions.

The 30th of June – When the enemy had reached the parish of *Beaumont*, on the southern coast four leagues from the town, a party of seven to eight hundred men made two feints beyond *Pointe de Lévy*, while the embarking troops advanced on the point. They were harassed along the roads for two leagues by about sixty Canadians, who sent one of their men to warn the *Général* of this first landing. The *Général* immediately sent about thirty savages who soon met the troops, firing on them around two o'clock in the afternoon. *Mr Dufils Charest*,[61] *sieur* of the *Pointe de Lévy*, and the *Sieur LeGris*,[62] officer of the militia, begged the *Général* to allow

59 François-Louis Poulin de Courval (1728–1769) Naval officer, native of Québec, trained as a river pilot in 1746 and began his naval career. 1752 he became captain of a merchant ship and made frequent trips between France and Canada. *Capitaine* of the *Bienfaisant* at Québec. André Lachance, 'Poulin de Courval, François-Louis,' in *Dictionary of Canadian Biography*, vol.3 (Toronto: University of Toronto/ Université Laval, 2003–).

60 The *Atalante*: 32-gun frigate commanded by Jean Vauquelin, senior French naval officer at the siege of Québec. *L'Atalante* would be burned in action on 17 May 1760. Campeau, *Navires Venus en Nouvelle-France*.

61 Joseph Charest (Charet) *dit* Dufils captain of *Le Soleil Royal*, 300 tons out of Bayonne. Lost 23 November 1759 at Sault la Chaudière. Campeau, *Navires Venus en Nouvelle-France*.

62 Pierre-Denis LeGris (1733–?). 'This Mr LeGris seems to have been active throughout the campaign in a very daring and useful role. He is often mentioned as a courier with dangerous missions or a fighter in the heart of it. ...' Anon., *Journal du Siège de Québec*, footnote 256, pp.98–99.

them to join the fight with about three hundred Canadians, savages and sailors, who offered to follow the officers, which they were granted. They had no sooner arrived than they engaged the enemy in a battle lasting from three o'clock until six, within sight of the city, our people having the upper hand and forcing the enemy from the battlefield, where the Indians had already taken a dozen scalps and one prisoner; *Mr Dufils Charest* wanted to press the advantage which he had just won, gathered the savages to induce them to increase the laurels with which they had just covered themselves, consequently he proposed to them to sleep on the field of battle, to send their prisoner back to the *Général*, that he would ask for a reinforcement of one thousand men to force the enemies to re-embark the next morning, to which the Indians willingly agreed, especially as they had none killed or wounded in this first battle. *Mr Dufils Charest* detached five or six savages to take their prisoner to the General. There the prisoner stated, if we are to believe him, that the enemy had made the descent at *Pointe de Lévy* only to attract our forces to this coast, to facilitate their descent at *Beauport*, which was to be attempted the next night; on the news of this first prisoner, the *Général* sent orders to the detachment at *Pointe de Lévy*, to the regret of the whole city, to join the army which spent the night in our entrenchments, that the enemy appear to have made no movement; the evacuation of *Mr Dufils Charest*'s detachment from the enemy's landing was made under cover of the terrain, and allowed them to retreat in secret.

The 1st of July – At eight o'clock in the morning *Mr Le Sage*, officer on the frigate *Le Senneterre*,[63] and *Mr Faucon*, officer of the frigate *Marcheault*, each commanding a division of four *jacobites* carrying an eight pound cannon,[64] left the coast of *Beauport*, drifting to the *Pointe de Lévy*, the enemy not suspecting that the boats could have guns, thought our people were coming to engage at their camp, quickly took to the edge of the wood, part feigning to resist to better attract our people, but they were very surprised when our *jacobite* boats, all in line, facing rifle troops which appeared on the edge of the wood, simultaneously fired their guns loaded with grape, continuing to load them for nearly half an hour, until two

63 *Le Maréchal de Senneterre*, 550 tons out of Bordeaux, captain: Joseph Goret de Grand Rivière *capitaine* de St-Malo. *Proprio*: La Tuilière & Cie. Campeau, *Navires Venus en Nouvelle-France*; Anon., *Journal du Siège de Québec*, p.91.

64 *Jacobite* boats are small open boats, similar to a ship's boat, armed with a single gun. '[July 27, 1758] Lieutenant Louis-Thomas Jacau (Jacault or Jacob) de Fiedmont of the Royal Artillery successfully fired a twelve-pound cannon from a gunboat of his own design. The year before Fiedmont had built and demonstrated a similar vessel, which mounted a twelve-pound cannon in its prow and two smaller swivel guns along the sides. Montcalm had been so pleased with the design, which despite its small size handled well when its armament was test fired, that he placed it at the head of his flotilla bound for the siege of Fort William Henry. The "Jacobs," as the gunboats were called, seem to have been little more than large *bateaux* with their prow and perhaps their stern cut so as to mount and handle the recoil of a nine or twelve-pound cannon.' Michael G. Laramie, 'The French Lake Champlain Fleet and the Contest for the Control of the Lake, 1742–1760', *Vermont History*, 80:1 (2012), pp. 1–32, p.5.

frigates detached from the fleet to hunt our *jacobite* boats, which retreated under the cannon of the city after having killed about one hundred men without loss or injury on our part.

The 2nd of July – The enemy raised a camp on the *Isle d'Orléans*, which they abandoned the same day. Several parties of savages passed over the island hoping to take some prisoners. *Mr Dufils Charest* with six to seven men passed the south coast to observe the enemy movements and to take notice of work they might have done. Having returned this evening, he reports that the enemy dug several redoubts for which they have now landed the guns, that their camp appeared to be three to four thousand men, and they raised two magazines on the edge of the wood to store their ammunition, finally they entrenched *le Petit Roché* to cover their camp.[65]

The 3rd of July – The enemy, numbering six or seven hundred, appeared opposite descending to the edge of the beach; several cannon shots were fired from the batteries of the lower town, which obliged them to return to the top of the shoreline, where they made an *abatis* of wood to build up their batteries.[66] From time to time the inhabitants and savage Mikmaques shot from their cover in the woods.

The 4th of July – The enemy made a great movement with their barges and appeared to land a large body of men and effects both at the *Isle d'Orléans* and at *Pointe de Lévy*, where their camps and works appear to have greatly increased. This evening they fired a first cannon shot to which their vessels replied; our army was under arms all night.

The 5th of July – About one hour after midday, a canoe with a white flag appeared, and at once the *Chevalier Bernetz*,[67] commander of the lower town, detached an officer escorted by four of our *carcassières* to meet the envoy.[68] The English officer

65 *Petit Roché* (*Anse à Petit*): topographical name in use since the 17th century in the parish of Sainte-Pétronille. Situated north of Fort Cove, Little Rock was designated for this area in 1657. Jean Poirier, 'La toponymie de l'Isle d'Orléans', *Cahiers de Géographie du Québec*, 6:12 (1962), pp.183–199, https://www.erudit.org/fr/revues/cgq/1962-v6-n12-cgq2586/020380ar.pdf (accessed 27 August 2018), p.196.

66 An abatis (abattis or abbattis) was made by felling trees before a defensive position, closely set with their branches facing outward and sharpened into spikes (Foligné uses 'abbatie').

67 Félicien de Bernetz, Chevalier (1705–?) Cadet in the Royal Roussillon 1725, *enseigne* 1726, *lieutenant* 1728, *capitaine* 1734, second commander 1755, *lieutenant colonel* 1756. After the fall of Québec, he returned to France. Knight of the Order of St John of Jerusalem. (Foligné uses 'Bernes'.) Government of Canada, 'Database of the 1759–1760 soldiers,' *The National Battlefields Commission: Plains of Abraham*, Government of Canada, http://www.ccbn-nbc.gc.ca/en/history-heritage/battles-1759-1760/soldiers/ (accessed 29 August 2018).

68 *Carcassières*: small boats mounted with guns to fire red-hot shot or incendiary shells. University of Chicago, 'Dictionnaire vivant de la langue Française', ARTFL Project, https://dvlf.uchicago.edu/ (accessed

produced a letter for *Mr de Vaudreuil*, the content of the letter, he says, is merely a courtesy from General Wolfe to our General,[69] to provide news of the three marine guards taken prisoner on the *Isle aux Coudres*, the exchange of which Mr Wolfe proposes for several of our ladies taken on the south coast; but it is presumed that this is only a pretext to examine our forces more closely.

The 6th of July – The *Chevalier Mercier* was dispatched to bear the letter from the General in reply to that from Mr Wolfe. A naval officer came to meet our envoy. The two canoes having met, the English officer led *Mr Mercier* aboard the flagship, then to General Wolfe to whom *Mr Mercier* handed the General's letter, could not say no to a cordial invitation to luncheon, the enemy offering all forms of politeness to him, in order to profit by the time they would converse with him. But our savages, perceiving a barge probing the channel north-east of the *Isle d'Orléans*, sent fifteen or twenty in a bark canoe and gave chase to the barge, that, before it could land, was so engaged that our savages scalped one of them while continuing to chase them to ground. They [the English] deployed five or six hundred men from the camp on the beach to cover their people, our savages, seeing the reinforcement, signaled to the canoes which had joined them to follow them. The stragglers in, they left a guard for their canoes, were attacked by the enemy, with whom they exchanged fire for an hour. A second enemy detachment forced our savages to re-embark, after killing a dozen men and injuring as many more, without loss. Consequently, this hostility forced *Mr Mercier* to return, reporting his full knowledge of the works which the enemy were making both at *Isle d'Orléans* and *Pointe de Lévy*.

The 7th of July – Fresh east winds, several ships anchored wanting to enter the *Sault Montmorency* channel by slipping up the *Beauport* coast, our floating battery is positioned on the shore of that coast and harries them in their maneuver, firing with much vivacity. The ships were no less lively, for more than an hour, until several of our *carcassières* and *jacobites* were detached from the harbor to come to the aid of our battery. Approaching the ships they opened a heavy fire, the ships returning fire from above our battery, chasing off our *carcassières*, letting themselves drift within range of the city's guns, where the ramparts fired so robustly that the ships returned to anchor among their fleet. Thus this fight ends without loss or damage on our part, we do not know the damage that the enemy had by our balls, which we saw well fired. This same day, *Mr de Vaudreuil* received a courier

8 September 2018); and '*Carcassière*', *Wiktionary*, https://www.wiktionary.org/ (accessed 3 July 2018).

69 Major General James Wolfe (1727–1759) Began his career in 1741 as a sub-lieutenant, 1742 ensign 12th Regiment of Foot, 1743 lieutenant, 1744 captain 4th of Foot, 1747 brigadier, 1748 major 20th of Foot, 1750 lieutenant colonel, 1757 colonel 67th of Foot, 1758 brigadier in America, 1759 major general. C.P. Stacey, 'Wolfe, James', in *Dictionary of Canadian Biography*, vol.3 (Toronto: University of Toronto/ Université Laval, 2003–).

from *Fort Duquesne* and was informed that our savages, five or six hundred in number, had surprised a convoy of seventeen wagons laden with war goods and provisions going to *Fort Cumberland*.[70] The escort had time to enter the fort.

The 8th of July – Between five and six o'clock in the morning, a deserter arrived at camp who reported that the enemy planned, in the coming night, to make a descent with three different attacks, one at *Sault de Montmorency* with four thousand men, another in the cove at *Beauport* with three thousand men, and a third in the lower town with a body of troops and sailors numbering four thousand, the latter will make their descent under cover of a cannonade from several war ships which will drop in front of the city. This same day, toward midday, a fully loaded *frégatte* and a *brigantin* passed through the *Sault Montmorency* channel and were anchored at *St Anne* without any difficulty,[71] an exercise the Canadians have not undertaken since the founding of the colony, fearing the pitfalls they saw overcome with ease.

The 9th of July – All our batteries in the city were fired with the utmost effort on the workers at *Pointe de Lévy*, where for several days the enemy have been building a battery to bombard the city. The quantity of bombs which the city throws up seemed to disturb them, by the flight which the workers take at one time or another. This same day, at three in the afternoon, forty to fifty barges loaded with troops joined their frigate and the *brigantin* anchored at *St Anne*, in favor of which they landed in the night a body of four thousand men with two cannon, without any opposition, and came to form their camp at the foot of the *Sault*, within a gunshot's distance of *Mr de Lévis*' camp. It was not without surprise seeing them in the morning, dug in, and to be joined by a body of troops coming from the *Isle d'Orléans*. The *Chevalier de Lévis* had no sooner seen the new enemy camp than he assembled the savages to engage them, to pass on the side of the enemy to harass them, before they were entirely retrenched, to which our savages consented, and set out with four hundred at six in the evening. The savages found themselves facing five hundred men who guarded over their workmen, fell on them with their tomahawks in their hands, and forced them to fall back to the bulk of their army with the loss of nearly one hundred men. Our savages, without loss, still animated by their first advantage, attacked the main body of the army, our savages were repulsed, hurried back wishing to give proofs to the generals of their first success, and, according to their custom, they wished to scalp the victims laid out from

70 *Fort Duquesne*: French fort built in 1754 at the junction of the Allegheny and Monongahela Rivers, at present-day Pittsburgh, Pennsylvania. *Fort Cumberland*: a crude frontier fort built by the Maryland militia in 1754 at the junction of the Potomac River and Wills Creek at present-day Cumberland, Maryland.

71 *Brigantin*: a two-masted ship with a square-rigged foremast and at least two sails on the main mast: a square topsail and a gaff sail mainsail behind the mast.

their first attack. When the enemy opposed them our savages lost fifteen dead or wounded; this loss cost the lives of five prisoners whom they had taken.

The 10th of July – One of their [the enemy's] batteries, set up in the night, began to fire on one of our redoubts in *Mr de Lévis'* camp, who was arranging twelve hundred men to attack the enemy when a ship with some frigates came to anchor at the channel of the *Sault* passage, which prevented the execution of the *Chevalier de Lévis'* project. This same day, between eight and nine o'clock in the morning, a *jacobite* boat intercepted a deserter who crossed from *Pointe de Lévy* to the city, who, having been led to our generals, stated that their army was composed of twelve thousand regulars, and twelve hundred men of the navy, and about fifteen hundred rangers, the two battalions of Royal Americans refused the service, that they had been re-embarked on the ships, in whose place they have landed a similar number of sailors who are sent to work on the south coast, that many of their soldiers waited only for an opportunity to desert. The *Marquis de Montcalm*, who occupies [commands] the center of our army, was no sooner informed of the new enemy camp at the *Sault* than he gave orders to the battalions of *La Sarre, Guyenne, Béarn*, and the *Trois Rivières* militia to establish a camp above the church in *Beauport*, where *Mr de Montcalm* came to camp, to help *Mr de Lévis* in case of attack; our vigilant general was occupied well into the night, to scout the different routes by which the enemy could pass; at the passage to the right of *Mr de Lévis'* camp was placed *Mr Duprat*,[72] Captain of *La Sarre*, commanding the volunteer regulars, along the woods *Mr Repentigny*, Captain of the Colony, commanding the militia volunteers. *Mr Charest*, who had spent the same day at the enemy's *Pointe de Lévy* camp, reports that the enemy now had eight guns of thirty-six pounds and as many mortars as they probably need landed on their battery, which targets the city, and which appeared to him almost ready to open. This same evening a detachment of our Abenaki savages returned to *Mr de Lévis'* camp, to whom they presented several scalps.

The 11th of July – At eight o'clock in the morning one of our Frenchmen arrived, having been made prisoner at the capture of *Louisbourg*, who afterward escaped from the vessels into the sea, who reported to the General that many of our Frenchmen were in the fleet, having been pressed into service, who only waited for the right moment to desert, that many foreigners whom the enemy had in their force hold the same sentiments, that they would rise up in their camp if a French fleet appeared on the river nearby. This same day a large quantity of war goods was received at *Mr de Lévis'* camp, which was immediately put to use by more than

72 Jean-Baptiste Duprat (1718–1760) officer of La Sarre regiment, later killed at the battle of St Foi. Entered service in 1736, sergeant 1737, 2nd lieutenant 1745, lieutenant 1745, captain 1754 (Foligné uses 'Dupras'). Government of Canada, 'Database of the 1759–1760 soldiers'.

two hundred cannon shots and bombs on those who served the artillery, which the enemy appeared to be putting in batteries, which when complete will soon fire on *Mr de Lévis'* camp, where our volunteers exchange gunshots continually with those of the enemy. All day, the city has maintained a keen fire on the enemy's workers in front of the city, but in a vain attempt to prevent the bombardment which will soon begin. This same evening the *Guyenne* regiment with about six hundred militiamen were occupied in marching on the approaches at the *Sault*, where at night we began to raise the escarpments,[73] toward breaking the enemy barrage of *Mr de Lévis'* camp, who have the advantage by the height they occupy. The first battalion, after twenty-four hours, to be relieved by another battalion, and so on alternately to the completion of the work on which the safety of our army will depend, in case the enemy wished to attempt their descent in this area.

The 12th of July – As yesterday, the enemy began a continual fire into *Mr de Lévis'* camp, who has withdrawn due to the bullets, bombs, and grenades which rain on his camp without much loss, amounting to six to seven men killed or wounded. This same day, at nine o'clock in the morning, the whole body of the *bourgeoisie*,[74] *Mr d'Oline*, Judge of *Québec* at the head, came to the camp for the third time to relate to the General what their loss would be if he did not allow them to make from among them a detachment of twelve to fifteen hundred men to go to *Pointe de Lévy* the next night in an effort to overthrow the enemy battery, which to them seems ready to open. The General thought it right to grant their just request, given their evident readiness to save their property in the city: consequently, *Mr Dumas*,[75] major general of the Colony troops, was ordered to take the command of this detachment which, by its appearances, was likely to cover itself with laurels by the opportunity with which the General has honored them, and the *bourgeoisie* were most satisfied to have an officer leading them whose bravery and prudence nearly all had witnessed. The *Marquis de Montcalm* wanted our regular troops to participate in the glory of this expedition as well and gave orders to the battalions of *La Sarre* and *Languedoc* to send two hundred volunteers, who served under the command of two lieutenants, to join the bulk of the detachment and to serve as an advanced guard. All things thus ordered, *Mr Dumas* left at night with fifteen

73 An escarpment is a steep slope fronting a fortification, designed to slow or thwart an enemy and to provide cover to the fortification.

74 The *bourgeoisie* were the members of the middle class, mostly property owners earning their living through business and commerce.

75 Jean-Daniel Dumas (1721–1794) officer of colonial regular troops, entering service in 1742, *lieutenant-en-second*, grenadier company 1743, fought in the Austrian War of Succession and named *capitaine* in 1747. Arrived in Canada in 1750, became an Indian negotiator and was posted at Fort Duquesne. Participated at the battle of the Monongahela, the taking of Fort William Henry, and in 1759 was named Adjutant General and inspector of colonial regular troops in Canada. Étienne Taillemite, 'Dumas, Jean-Daniel', in *Dictionary of Canadian Biography*, vol.4 (Toronto: University of Toronto/Université Laval, 2003–).

hundred men to go to *Cap Rouge*, where there were *bâteaux* to cross. When he arrived, he crossed with all his people, from which he assigned about fifty men to guard the *bâteaux*, formed his detachment into two columns, and with the benefit of a most obscure night he advanced to the house of *Bourassard*, one league from the battery. There *Mr Dumas* halted and sent some inhabitants and savages to scout. On their return, without having seen anything, our detachment again took up their march, but the guides were gone. Fortunately, during a second halt, eighty inhabitants of *Pointe de Lévy* joined *Mr Dumas*, knowing the terrain perfectly, calmed *Mr Dumas* who wanted to get back on the road. They were detected by some Canadian stragglers who found them along a fence, believed themselves in front of the enemy, in fear they took flight which caused panic in the center of the detachment who fired their guns and caused such a rout that *Mr Dumas* was unable to rally his men, fearing the enemy would be attracted by this shooting and come to the location he thought it prudent to withdraw with the troops not part of the disorder, and returned to the *bâteaux* where he found two-thirds of his detachment embarked who were firing randomly. Only with difficulty could he get them to land, reproaching them for their weakness. Such was the expedition of our brave citizens of *Québec*, who eight days past complained loudly that the General did not allow them to secure their city from the bombardment; it would have been more honorable for the nation, and more glorious for *Mr Dumas*, if the General would have continued to refuse them; we had but two men killed and five to six wounded. This same evening they [the British] fired a *fuzé*[76] on board their flagship,[77] which was the signal for the bombardment of the battery established for this effect. One quickly followed by another, and in the moment they began the bombardment supported by a strong cannonade. The enemy continued this play throughout the night, there being a great deal of shelling, while not diminishing the fire from the enemy batteries, which caused us no loss.

The 13th of July – In the dark of night a *galliote à bombe* came to anchor before the city, after firing several shots to which our own gunners responded from the ramparts with such accuracy, and our cannoneers from the batteries of the lower town fired so lively, that the galley was forced to retire. Today the enemy did not fire heavily on the city. This same day the nuns of the city were at the hospital.[78]

76 A *fuzé* (*fusée*) was a signal rocket or flare.

77 HMS *Neptune*, Rear Admiral Saunders' flagship. Built at Portsmouth, England in 1757, it had three decks and 90 guns, built 171 feet in length and 48 feet six inches in beam. Anon., 'HMS Neptune (1757),' *Wikipedia*, www.wikipedia.com (accessed 27 August 2018).

78 Foligné refers to the relocation of the Augustinian Sisters of *Hôtel Dieu* and the Ursulines from their city-center convents to shelter at the General Hospital, out of range of the British guns.

The 14th of July – This day one of our parties of savages returned with five scalps taken at the enemy camp at *Sault Montmorency*, which had been sending a very lively fire onto *Mr de Lévis*' camp.

The 15th of July – The enemy in front of the town continued a lively bombardment of the place; one of their carcasses, sent at about eleven o'clock in the morning, set fire to *Madame la Naudière*'s house, which spread to four other houses.[79] This same day we had one of our cannons knocked down.

From the 16th to the 17th the fire from the ramparts was most lively, to the benefit of our people busy fighting the fire which was finally stopped, and which spread no further. The rest had been saved.

The 17th of July – The enemy bombarded the city, we had a gun at the *Batterie Dauphine* dismounted and two men killed. The enemy fire at the *Sault* was no less severe. It appears that this area is where they wish to make their attack, having about thirty-five to forty guns there. This same day a party of eighty or one hundred savages left the city with some Canadians, commanded by *Mr Hertel*,[80] lieutenant of the colony, and in the morning they attacked an enemy party at the *Sault*, luring them into one of their best-led ambushes; in the morning, unknown to the enemy, they had sent a detachment of around 150 men to set an ambuscade, then several Canadians were sent across the plain. Once detected they feinted to the edge, as if to save themselves, to the point where the savages were lying in wait. When the ambush was sprung the enemy were not able to reverse, the savages charging them tomahawk in hand, the enemy with shocked faces. They retreated after losing thirty to forty men, and three of their people taken prisoner, who report that General Wolfe with a body of troops numbering nine to ten thousand men, will soon try to force the area where they are currently carrying artillery, that

79 Louise-Geneviève de La Naudière, wife of Charles-François Tarieu de La Naudière and daughter of Henri-Louis Deschamps de Boishébert. Prominent Québec socialite whose salon was popular among the elite of Québec society. Montcalm once referred to their own relationship as being 'the best of friends'. (Foligné uses 'Nodière'.) Marie-Céline Blais, 'Tarieu de La Naudière, Charles-François,' in *Dictionary of Canadian Biography*, vol.4 (Toronto: University of Toronto/ Université Laval, 2003–).

80 Étienne Hertel, also referred to as Hertel the Elder or Eldest. French cadet at Fort St Frédéric aged 14. 1749 ordered to serve at Louisbourg, promoted *enseigne-en-second* 1751, *enseigne* in 1755, 1757 he was recalled to Michilimackinac and in 1759 he was named *lieutenant* at Vaudreuil's recommendation. 'Knowing his ascendancy over the Indians he had been reminded to put him in charge of the parties working to prevent Wolfe's army from crossing the Montmorency River.' This action is not specifically mentioned in the document, but a 26 July *sortie* is included. Thomas Charland, 'Les neveux de Madame de Beaubassin', *Revue d'Histoire de l'Amérique Française*, 23:1 (June 1969), p.72, https://www.erudit.org/en/journals/haf/1969-v23-n1-haf2070/302854ar/ (accessed 27 August 2018); and C.J. Russ, 'Hertel de Saint-François, Étienne,' in *Dictionary of Canadian Biography*, vol.3 (Toronto: University of Toronto/ Université Laval, 2003–).

they had withdrawn all their regular troops from *Pointe de Lévy* to their camp at the *Sault*, with the exception of four to five hundred who remained to cover their battery, that they had since been cut off from food, which they had sent three packets for *Louisbourg* to fetch,[81] that lastly, they waited day by day to be joined by General Amherst's army.

The 18th of July – The city did not receive much damage from the enemy fire, which was much slower; this day, in the afternoon, a courier arrived from *Montréal* carrying letters from *Carillon* and *Niagara*; *Mr Bourlamaque*,[82] *Brigadier Commandant* of our army at *Carillon*, composed of about four thousand men, notes to our generals that his works are finished and he calmly awaits the enemy, from whom deserters arrive each day, who state that General Amherst – with an army of fifteen to twenty thousand men camped for some days at Fort George, intends to leave at any moment to attack our entrenchments at *Carillon*. *Mr Pouchot*,[83] *commandant* at *Fort Niagara*, states they are besieged since the 6th instant of the current month, by five to six thousand men, but is able to hold out until help he has requested from *Detroit* and *Belle Rivière* arrives, necessary if he hopes to raise the siege, which makes our generals seem at ease for this part.

The 19th of July – At about nine or ten o'clock at night, a small [English] fleet in the north-east, a fresh wind, one vessel of fifty-four guns with two frigates, taking advantage of a very obscure night, passed before the town, and though well-served the fire from the ramparts could not prevent them, firing randomly. A third frigate of 24 guns ahead of them ran aground on the shoal off *Pointe de Lévy*, where the enemy work hard to unload it. Several of our *carcassières*, having noticed them, wanted to inconvenience them in their work, but several cannons, already mounted on land, forced our *carcassières* to withdraw. Despite the heavy

81 Packet-boats were medium sized ships chartered for specific uses or assigned regular communication routes between points, carrying mail, passengers, or goods.

82 François-Charles de Bourlamaque (1716–1764) Entered service as a volunteer in 1739, *lieutenant-en-second* 1740, *lieutenant* 1742, *capitaine aide-major* 1745, *capitaine* 1745. Participated in the Austrian War of Succession. 1756 dispatched to Canada as a *colonel* and third in command. Present at Oswego, Fort Ontario, Fort William Henry, the defense of Carillon, and commanded at the time of the French withdrawal from Carillon. (Foligné uses 'le Boug de la Mare'.) C.P. Stacey, 'Bourlamaque, François-Charles de', in *Dictionary of Canadian Biography*, vol.3 (Toronto: University of Toronto/Université Laval, 2003–).

83 Pierre Pouchot (Pouchot de Maupas, Pouchat, Pourchaut, Boucheau) (1712–1769) Military engineer, officer. Entered service at 21 as volunteer engineer, *lieutenant-en-second* Béarn 1734, served at Corsica, Italy, Flanders, and Germany, made *capitaine* in 1749. Sent to Canada 1755 and served at Fort Frontenac and Fort Niagara. At Oswego, Montréal, and a short time at Carillon before taking the post as commander at Niagara. 1757 promoted to *lieutenant colonel*, in October replaced as commander at Niagara. 1758 he was at the defense of Carillon with Béarn, defending the right flank of the breastwork against the British Highlanders. March 1759 he returned to Niagara as its commander. Peter N. Moogk, 'Pouchot, Pierre', in *Dictionary of Canadian Biography*, vol.3 (Toronto: University of Toronto/Université Laval, 2003–).

fire of the enemy there was no great damage to the city. The ships, after passing the city and cannonading one of our fireships, and seeing no one was aboard, sent a barge to set it on fire. *Mr le Jeune*,[84] commanding a *carcassière*, left from *l'Anse des Mères* and gave chase to the barge,[85] came within range and fired on it, but in vain as the heat of the burning ships forced him to retire, abandoning our fireship, and to let it burn; the same barge came down to set fire to two of our *bâteaux*. *Mr Courval*, having noticed this, hid himself with some of his sailors in the edge of the wood, allowed the enemy to approach within range, and after a quick volley from their guns the barge was obliged to sail off, but in the middle of the night they succeeded in taking our two *bâteaux*.

The 20th of July – At ten o'clock in the morning three [blank space] barges set off from the cape opposite *l'Anse des Mères*, where *Mr le Jeune* saw them and set out with his *carcassière* and a *jacobite* boat to give chase. He closed in on them, forcing them to run aground after hitting a barge and killing five men. In the morning of that same day *Mr Mercier* took several pieces of artillery opposite the vessels where there was a battery of 2 cannon and a mortar, fired and forced the frigates to sail up higher, and the big ship to drop into the protected area. This whole time our gunners continued to dispatch shells, forcing the ship leading this fleet to go up with the *frégattes* to *Cap Rouge*, where *Mr Dumas*, with about two hundred men, saw them along this coast. Two other guns already on the way to be placed in the new battery there were quickly mounted and the ships were driven back to the city. At four o'clock that same afternoon a deserter came in from the enemy camp at the *Sault*, who states that the frigate stranded the day before can be freed without damage. His statement is verified later that evening, when the enemy drew the frigate off. Some savages spent this morning at the enemy camp at the *Sault*, arrived back after sunset not having been able to take a prisoner or a scalp, the enemy having refused to engage; the heavy enemy fire in front of the city lasted all day but did no damage.

From the 20th to the 21st, over six night-time hours, the enemy before the city opened a new battery of several guns and three mortars, standing to the north-east of their first. All night they fired broadly and caused some damage in the remote districts. The enemy forces in this area lack food and in consequence had begun rationing, reduced to a half-pound of bread or flour and half a pound of meat. They gave no food to the detachments which they sent daily to scavenge in

84 There are two possible candidates. Ambroise Lejeune (1718–1800) Arrived in Canada as a recruit in 1738, unknown rank in Troupes de la Marine; or Gérard Lejeune (1727–1768) Arrived in Canada 1750, unknown rank in Troupes de la Marine. 'Database of the 1759-1760 soldiers,' *The National Battlefields Commission: Plains of Abraham.*

85 *L'Anse des Mères*: Mothers' Cove, just SW of Cape Diamond and below the Plains of Abraham.

the countryside. Several of their big ships crossed to come broadsides a little before the city. This same day the *Marquis de Montcalm* went to *Mr de Lévis*' camp and to the edge of our entrenchments, which, at that time, he recognized as such that he would not fear enemy batteries or General Wolfe, their opponent, who had a great volley fired in the presence of our General, to cries of joy from our working soldiers, which resounded to the enemy's camp: *Mr de Montcalm*, having made sure of our retrenchments, gave an order to *Mr de Lévis* to take possession of the land which his troops occupied before the enemy had batteries in this part, and the battalions of *La Sarre*, *Languedoc*, *Béarn*, and the militia currently camped at the church in *Beauport* are to return to reoccupy their previous position, where our General will establish his quarters and where the General and the Intendant currently camped. This same evening the enemy sent back the women they had taken in an earlier landing on *Pointe aux Trembles*,[86] and demanded a cessation of arms for the next day until midday so that their sick could be removed, which our generals granted them; despite the great fire of the enemy at *Pointe de Lévy*, the city did not suffer seriously.

From the 22nd to the 23rd a very heavy night bombardment by the enemy set fire to the upper town, near *Madame la Gue*, which was spread by a NW wind to the Cathedral after having burned thirteen houses: throughout the night they threw a quantity of bombs, firebombs and *carcasses*, in the area of the fire, which was fortunately cut off from spreading by the houses of the first fire, which saved the Bishop's house and the seminary; the battery here was forced to remove the powders and bombs which were threatened by the sparks which fell there in great quantity. Near sunrise a *frégatte* of twenty-six guns and a *galliote à bombe* advanced to pass under cover of the fire, but – being seen from the ramparts – we fired on them and forced them back to anchor with their fleet.

The 23rd of July – At seven o'clock in the morning the enemy passed several *bâteaux* in front of the city as a result of the permission they had obtained the day before, but instead of the sick whom they were to conduct to their camp on *Isle d'Orléans* it was food and cattle taken during their landing at *Pointe aux Trembles*: all that day they did not shoot on the city, one assumes they reveled in the fire they caused the night before.

The 24th of July – The enemy continued the bombardment, one of their bombs started a fire which was immediately extinguished: in spite of the large quantity of bombs that they fired the remainder of the night, estimated to have been

86 *Pointe aux Trembles* was approximately halfway between *Cap Santé* and Québec City on the shores of the Rivière St Laurent. Site of present-day Neuville, Québec.

A View of the Bishop's House with the Ruins, Québec, 1759, etching by Richard Short, copied 1863 by William Notman. (McCord Museum, I-6410.1)

two hundred and fifty, certainly a low estimate of shots, the city was not much damaged.

The 25th of July – The *Chevalier Mercier*, commander of artillery, represented to the General that it would be expedient to find an excuse for procuring a truce, during which time they would work on platforms and re-mounting the cannons dismounted by the bombs and cannonballs of the enemy, to which the General happily agreed, *Mr Mercier*'s request being for the good of the service. Consequently our generals took the opportunity to reply to Mr Wolfe's politeness, who had sent them a few cases of liquor which in truth had cost the English the trouble of taking one of our ships. *Mr Mercier* was sent to express our generals' gratitude, who, in return, sent to the Admiral and to General Wolfe several bottles of wine and liqueurs. The *Chevalier Mercier* was to gain as much time as was possible; he left from the square at ten o'clock in the morning. As soon as the enemy perceived *Mr Mercier*'s *bâteau* the flagship detached an officer in the front who, having joined *Mr Mercier*, proposed to take him on board the *Neptune*, where, after having arrived, *Mr Mercier* was so cautious about his embassies, that he provided all the time necessary for the works which had been planned; our officers scattered on the different batteries, scurried busily all the time of the truce, they put everyone to work repairing platforms and remounting the cannon, after which they wanted to raise the embankments of their batteries, were seen in their labors by the enemy, who scarcely waited for the return of *Mr Mercier* with the flag of truce, when the enemy recommenced their fire with two rockets, eight to ten bombs, reassured by the discharge of their cannon and continued so all night. Toward ten o'clock one of their fire-pots set two houses alight in the upper town, in the *Récollets* district.[87] While they worked to extinguish the fire, this part of the city received a quantity of bombs and *carcasses* that did not have the same result; this third fire did not spread.

This same night the enemy, having learned of several of our *carcassières* between *Sillery* and *Cap Rouge*, detached a *frégatte* of 26 guns and a *bâteau* of six to surprise our *carcassières*. Consequently, they descended from *Pointe aux Trembles* to *Cap Rouge* to engage our *carcassières*, the officers of which not foreseeing the designs of the frigate and the *bâteau*, left *Cap Rouge* to follow their orders, which were to go and observe the enemy at *Pointe aux Trembles*. At daybreak they saw a ship and two frigates tack toward shore, just as three of our *jacobite* boats, fearing attack, when rounding the tip of *Cap Rouge* they saw the frigate and the *bâteau* heading for them with about eight to ten barges. At once they [the French commanders of the *jacobite* boats] ordered the men to lie down, awaited the approach of the ships to within a rifle-shot before firing their artillery, which they later spiked and retreated into the edge of the wood, forced off by the sharp fire of the frigate which saw our people fleeing and detached the *bâteau* which came to clear the area; drawing within a pistol's shot and putting a sailor on board one of the *jacobite* boats, there wasn't time to guide the boat alongside the frigate or sink it; a short time later the enemy set out to take a *carcassière*, with our one officer and twelve sailors to oppose them. He [the officer] awaited the return of another officer who had gone after deserting sailors and was returning with what sailors he could reach as well as some Canadians, joining our ambushed people just as the enemy landed several barges under the protective fire of the frigate. Our people repulsed them with such vigor that they returned to their ships with the loss of about forty men and one of their sailors taken prisoner, while we had an officer slightly wounded. In the end our people re-embarked after which the frigate returned to anchor, the prisoner not wishing to embark was put into the hands of some of the savages who had come at the sound of the fusillade, but continuing to revolt in the hands of these men, at last was scalped.

The 26th of July – After bombing the city as usual, at 3 p.m. the enemy returned several women taken on the southern coast, which stopped the fire on both sides in this area, while at the *Sault* the enemy tried with a body of two thousand men

87 *Récollets*: a French reform branch of the Franciscans. Récollets took vows of poverty and devoted their lives to prayer and penance, as well as missionary work.

to force the ford where our volunteers held on firmly,[88] waiting for the help they expected to come from *Mr de Lévis*' camp, who detached about six hundred men with our savages who arrived in time to force the enemy to withdraw after a loss of thirty men and twenty on our part.

The 27th of July – The enemy opened a third battery at *Pointe de Lévy* that pounded the city near the palace without much damage, despite their lively fire all day. This same evening *Mr Le Gris*, a merchant of *Québec*, arrived with three prisoners from *Pointe de Lévy*, where he had been for two days. The prisoners report that the enemy were now 4,000 men at their camp at *Pointe de Lévy*, they plan a landing at *Sillery*, which they must take to ravage our shores, and that they wish for the arrival of Mr Amherst. A deserter who arrived tonight is reporting the same thing.

The 28th of July – *Mr Courval* was ordered to take command of the *cajeux* which, for a few days, they [the French commanders] had been planning to send against the [British] fleet.[89] All things being ready, *Mr Courval* departed from *l'Anse des Mères* toward nine o'clock in the evening, at the start of the ebb tide, with quite fresh south-west winds. As they passed before the city many of our *carcassières* destined to support them joined in. *Mr Courval* maintained his route until he felt it was time to release the fire rafts. He lit them at about ten o'clock in the evening, they passed through the fleet, where they ignited two ships, but the prompt response from the other vessels succeeded in extinguishing the fires; all night the enemy sent a quantity of bombs, balls, *carcasses* and fire-pots, which did not cause considerable damage.

The 29th of July – At the moment a *chaloupe* set off from beside the flagship the enemy raised the truce flag at the center of the *Pointe de Lévy* battery. The *Chevalier Bernetz*, commander of the lower town, immediately met with an English officer, who, after having turned over several women and a letter from General Wolfe to *Mr de Vaudreuil*, whose response he would come back to retrieve, returned to his ship. The truce continued until the *Général* had prepared his reply to the letter he had just received, in which Mr Wolfe complained of the cruelties which our Indians and Canadians were committing, to which the *Général* replied that he was assured that the Canadians had not been scalping, that the Indians did he was not surprised, and more so that it was a custom of theirs that he must not ignore;

88 Malartic identifies this location as 'the winter ford'. On the 1759 Plan of Québec published by E. Oakley, the ford is indicated by dotted lines and marked as being guarded by two eight-gun hulks placed in the mouth of the St Charles River. William Raffle (ed.), *Glories to Useless Heroism: The American Journals of Comte Maurès de Malartic, 1755–1760* (Solihull: Helion & Company, 2017), p.226; and 'A Plan of Québec', *Massachusetts Historical Society: Maps of the French and Indian War*, http://www.masshist.org/maps/27Atlas16Quebec/27Atlas16Quebec.htm (accessed 30 August 2018).

89 *Cajeux* are fire rafts.

the truce ended at six o'clock in the evening, after which the enemy began the bombardment more vigorously than they had done before. Nothing remarkable near the Sault or the enemy, for two or three days sending a number of bombs and grenades on our camp without causing any damage.

The 30th of July – A deserter arrived from *Pointe de Lévy* camp who reported that some frigates would try a landing on the coast near *Sillery*, that, consequently, there were at present about sixty barges at *Pointe de Lévy* for the embarkation of their troops, which are to sail the following night, along the south coast to join the vessels which are to draw up in front of *Sillery*. This same day the *Marquis de Montcalm*, accompanied by *Mr de Bougainville* and several officers of the different battalions, went to the city where he toured the ramparts from which there was a lively firing while they visited the works, after having examined them and given his orders, he left the city to come to the General Hospital where he passed through every room visiting the wounded, whom he gave wine, after which he returned to the camp. That same evening, about nine to ten o'clock, a very heavy firing on the city started, which led one to believe that they [the British] had actually begun a landing. All night the city stood on guard in the entrenchments, but needlessly as the enemy made no move.

The 31st of July – At nine o'clock in the morning, at low tide and in south-westerly winds, calm seas, a ship of sixty-four and two frigates ran the channel north of *Isle d'Orléans*, across from the *Sault*. Half an hour later two other frigates tried to sail in and give a broadside at one of our redoubts. They ran aground in the low tide, then began a very active fire, so that the big ships and two other frigates, directing their fire sometimes on our redoubt, sometimes on *Mr de Lévis*' camp, their ground batteries or along the coast numbered more than forty guns, were no less well-served, but they fired in vain trying to turn out *Mr de Lévis*' camp, who had become accustomed to the sound of artillery for nearly a month. At ten o'clock about one hundred and fifty barges appeared alongside the vessels of the fleet, with three to four divisions making different movements. At midday one division, after having run along the north side of *Isle d'Orléans*, reached the main ship where she lay to. The other two divisions seemed to want to join the first, sometimes they seemed to want to disembark at the Canadian entrenchments. Finally, around five o'clock, they came together. They made a landing this side of the passage at the *Sault*, and by assault took the redoubt on which they had directed their fire since the morning; this first party was no sooner disembarked and ranged in battle lines than General Wolfe arrived at the end of the passage with about four thousand men, appearing to support the attack of the landed troops, numbering about three thousand, were about to try. The *Marquis de Montcalm*, having seen the morning movements of the enemy, gave orders to the grenadiers with a picket of each battalion to march to the *Sault*, where he had returned in the morning to the acclamations of joy by the whole camp, which proved to our *Général* the good

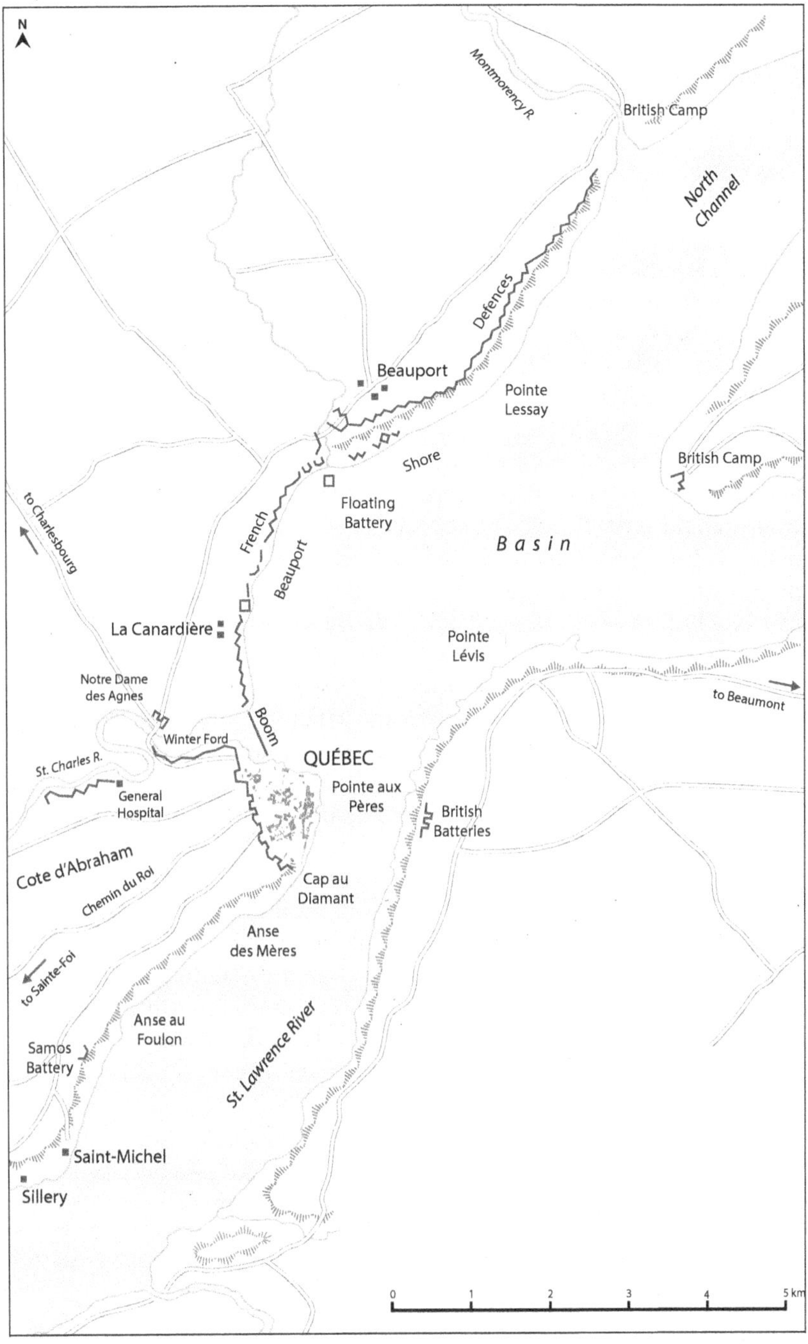

Map 3 Québec and Environs.

will of the whole throng to do their duty well. On arrival at *de Lévis*' camp, the *Marquis de Montcalm* immediately saw to the disposition of all the troops and to prepare everything; after which he summoned the Indians to engage them to post outside the entrenchments in the area of the advanced redoubt, so as to be able to better attract the enemy within range of our entrenchments.

At six o'clock the weather became rainy. The enemy landed and came forward with small arms and a resolute step, closing on our redoubt, where our troops had orders to retreat to the entrenchments, to gradually spike the cannon, and let the savages harass the enemy, after which the enemy could be better engaged. The enemy were not masters of our first redoubt for long, and seemed uneasy at the shooting of our savages, felt they should have profited by their first advantage and advanced toward our entrenchments. There within rifle-shot, *Mr de Montcalm* challenged them well, at which they ceased their advance, and returned to re-embark, which they did in good order. Our general immediately had our troops out of the entrenchments, advancing their bayonets, wanting to profit from the advantage that the enemy left him. Unfortunately a large storm having risen, our troops could only engage the rear of the enemy, who fired, suffering after a loss of nearly nine hundred men killed, wounded or drowned, and an officer with fifteen grenadiers taken prisoner. Our loss amounts to about thirty men killed or wounded including seven to eight savages. The enemy on the frigate seeing the failed attack on the *Sault*, did not see their troops re-embarked. Fearing being attacked themselves, they set fire to the *frégatte* from which our people saved a quantity of flour, bacon, spears, pickaxes and other digging tools. All this day and part of the night the batteries of *Pointe de Lévy* fired heavily. I'm told that between the two sides more than four thousand shots had been fired this day.

The 1st of August – We had one of the rampart mortars crushed by a bomb: the English officer wounded the day before was carried to the General Hospital this morning, after coming to he asked the favor of seeing the soldier who had saved his life the day before. The generosity of our *Guyenne* soldier is really worthy of being reported. During the battle our soldier, seeing the wounded officer and one of our savages, to whom he had just given his watch, about to scalp the officer, the soldier jumped on the savage and fought with him until our officers had removed the wounded man, who realized he owed his life to this brave soldier, whom he wished to see;[90] no sooner was he brought to him than he showed him his gratitude

90 Captain David Ochterlony, grenadier of the Royal Americans. Recently wounded in a duel with a German officer, he was shot through the lungs during the second British charge of the Battle of Montmorency, alongside Lieutenant Peyton who was shot through the leg. His men wanted to remove him from the field but he refused, Peyton then refused to abandon his captain. Robbed of his valuables Ochterlony was clubbed with a musket and shot, a savage approaching with his scalping knife as Lieutenant Peyton crawled to a nearby weapon and shot one native, then defended himself with his dagger from a second. A British rescue party arrived and carried Peyton back to the boats. Ochterlony was left for dead. Natives returned intent on scalping him, but the Guyenne soldiers had arrived and realized Ochterlony was still

and begged him to accept some guineas. The soldier paused, thanked him and stated it had been his pleasure to help. The *Général*, knowing the English officer had asked the soldier to accept a reward, sent *Mr de St Sauveur*,[91] his secretary, to the hospital, who after having explained the *Général* was aware of his situation and the offer of a reward, and he begged him not to worry about the reward, they would take care of the soldier. The English officer, after begging *Monsieur de St Sauveur* to express his gratitude to our generals for their gracious offer, begged them to allow him to write to his general reporting the generosity of the French soldier, our generals consented for the tranquility of that gentleman, after expressly forbidding the soldier to receive anything.

The 2nd of August – *Mr de St Laurent*, the *aide-major* of *Québec*, carrier of the wounded officer's letter, left the city at one o'clock.[92] The whole time of this truce was employed in repairing the damage which the enemy's fire had caused on our rampart batteries. *Mr de St Laurent* returned at five o'clock in the evening, after which the enemy recommenced the bombardment, their fire in the *Sault* was normal.

The 3rd of August – The enemy appeared to be making a great movement by transporting their troops from *Pointe de Lévy* to their *Sault* camp where, at two o'clock, they formed their troops in battle lines, pretending to take their revenge for the 13th [*sic*]. This farce set our army at arms, the city was bombed as was normal.

The 4th of August – The enemy were mostly quiet at the *Sault*, they were less so at *Pointe de Lévy* where they fired more than ever, sent bombs, fire-pots and *carcasses*, continuing so all night with a lively firing. We had six men killed, one wounded, and one cannon dismounted.

The 5th of August – The enemy near the *Sault* fired the most intense bombardment for half an hour in order to facilitate the desertion of one of our soldiers, whom they saw coming to them, who did so in spite of the great number of cannon shots

alive, one saving him by driving off the natives at the point of his *bayonette*. Ochterlony was carried to the French General Hospital where he was nursed by the nuns. Arthur Doughty and George W. Parmelee (eds.), *The Siege of Quebec and the Battle of the Plains of Abraham* (6 vols), vol.6 (Québec: Dessault & Proulx, 1901), p.337; and Robert Tomes, *Battles of America By Sea and Land*, vol.1 (New York: Virtue & Company, 1861), p.118.

91 André Grasset de Saint-Sauveur (1724–1794) merchant, secretary to Governor-General Vaudreuil. André Lachance, 'Grasset de Saint-Sauveur, André', *Dictionary of Canadian Biography*, vol.4 (Toronto: University of Toronto/ Université Laval, 2003–).

92 Most likely this is Louis-Joseph-Guillaume Gaillard De Saint-Laurent (1737–?). 1756 cadet in the artillery of the Colony Troops, 1758 *enseigne* in Guyenne, 1759 *lieutenant*. Returned to France with his regiment following the surrender of Québec. Guillaume Gaillard, 'La Famille Gaillard de Saint-Laurent', *Le Bulletin Des Recherches*, vol.41:1935, p.14, http://collections.banq.qc.ca/jrn03/dn2087/src/1935/04/164865_1935-04.txt (accessed 11 December 2018).

fired from our batteries. This same day the enemy at *Pointe de Lévy* continued to fire upon the city with the same vigor as the night before, directing their fire on the lower town, where we had about ten men killed or wounded and two officers.

The 6th of August – About two o'clock in the afternoon came a white-flagged *chaloupe*, and the *Chevalier Bernetz* immediately detached an officer to whom the English officer handed a letter from their general in response to that of the wounded officer, and a trunk for him. This little truce served to repair the damage to our batteries. From 6 to 7 in the night twenty five to thirty barges passed in front of the city and in response the General was beaten;[93] Immediately the battery soldiers set off to station at the powder-magazine, and about two hundred Canadians came out of the city to go and carry it to *l'Anse au Foulon*.[94] The *Marquis de Montcalm* set out with some of the grenadier companies when, at the bridge, news reached him that the barges had rejoined their vessels anchored at *Cap Rouge* with no sign of other movements. *Mr de Montcalm* came back.

The 7th of August – At ten o'clock in the morning a courier arrived from *Montréal*, charged with the letters from *Mr de Bourlamaque*, from whom we learned of the evacuation of *Carillon*, and our army, dug in at *Isle aux Noix*,[95] after having blown up the fortifications of Forts *Carillon* and *St Frédéric*.[96] This same day there was a great barrage in general and of the different camps. Our losses amount to fifteen men killed or wounded, those of the enemy are unknown. The firing from our ramparts, after having paused two to three times as had the enemy's), leaves us to think that they are not without loss.

The 8th of August – Six or seven barges joined the vessels below the town, attempted a landing at *Pointe aux Trembles*, but were strongly repulsed, and returned on board their ships; this same day fifteen to twenty inhabitants from *l'Ange Gardien* challenged an enemy party of about one hundred and fifty men who had taken two or three hundred cattle from the countryside;[97] our inhabitants, after forcing the enemy to abandon their catch, took the cattle back into the depths of the woods. All day the bombardment and all else were ordinary, without loss.

The 9th of August – The enemy, after having launched a large quantity of bombs, fire-pots and *carcasses* during the night, at three a.m. focused at two different

93 The General is one of a standard set of drum calls designed to convey information to the army. In the case of The General being beaten, all soldiers would prepare for an immediate march or engagement.

94 *L'Anse au Foulon*: Fuller's Bay – Between l'Anse des Mères and Samos Battery.

95 *Isle aux Noix*: Nut Island, located south of St John on the Richelieu River.

96 *Fort St Frédéric*: massive stone fortress, today a ruin, begun by the French in 1734, near present-day Crown Point, New York.

97 *L'Ange Gardien*: between Sault Montmorency and Beaupré.

places in the lower town, first at the *Cul de Sac*,[98] and secondly toward the *Batterie Dauphine*, with no chance of breaching it. The south-westerly winds, after falling to the north-west, caused a spreading fire in which there were one hundred and fifty houses burned. During the fire an enemy bomb blew up a powder chest on the rampart battery containing two hundred 18 pounder cartridges. Fortunately the one hundred men on this battery were unharmed. This same day some Canadians from *St Antoine*'s parish on the south coast took three prisoners, who state that there were currently one thousand marines and sailors in the camp, one hundred and fifty rangers and several pickets of regular troops, that the next night they will make an attempt at *Pointe aux Trembles*.

The 10th of August – At ten o'clock in the morning an order arrived from *Mr de Bougainville*'s camp which reports that at 2 o'clock in the morning the enemy, at low tide, tried a landing at *Pointe aux Trembles* with 27 barges. But *Mr de Bougainville* had ordered his men to lay on their arms along the coast, and to fire only at an agreed upon signal. This plan was closely executed by the troops, so that the enemy was within half a rifle's shot at its execution and unable to sustain against the great fire aimed upon them, returned and re-embarked without firing a shot, and at trying to make a second landing at a lower place they had been served the same as at the first. In the end they returned to their lines with the loss of nearly one hundred men, and twelve men killed or wounded on our part. All this day the city fired a great deal on the batteries, the enemy only responded with occasional fire; nothing remarkable happened in the *Sault* where both sides are on alert.

The 11th of August – A detachment of six to seven hundred Canadians and savages commanded by *Messieurs Hertel and Fleurimont Denoyelle*,[99] Colony officers, passed the *Sault* to go and surprise a body of the enemy, which the *Chevalier de Lévis* knew to be detached to run this coast; they caught up with them at midday, attacked them and drove them to their entrenchments after having killed about thirty men, whose scalps the savages carried to *Mr de Lévis*. Our loss was five men. This same day a courier arrived from *Montréal* reporting that *Mr Pouchot*, *commandant* at *Fort Niagara*, had capitulated on the twenty-seventh of last month, after a final summons, in which he knew positively that the enemy had captured two Huron savages carrying a letter from *Mr de Lignery*,[100] by which this *Monsieur* made it known the day he would arrive to reinforce the fort with nine hundred

98 *The Cul de Sac*: small cove at the west end of the lower town, beside the Royal Battery.

99 Charles-Joseph Denoyelle de Fleurimont (1719–1767) Troupes de la Marine: *enseigne-en-second* 1744, 1st *enseigne* 1749, *lieutenant* 1756. Government of Canada, 'Database of the 1759–1760 soldiers'.

100 François-Marie le Marchand de Lignery (1703–1759) *capitaine* in colonial regular troops. Relinquished Fort Duquesne in 1758, moved to Fort Machault at Venango (Franklin, PA). Abandoning plans for an attack on Fort Pitt, de Lignery marched to Pouchot's aid at Fort Niagara. As mentioned in the journal his letter with details of his advance was intercepted by the British, an ambush was set for 24 July, where he

men, but that the enemy with three thousand men supported by the savages of the Five Nations cut off the rescuers, fighting at the large meadow two leagues distant. After a lively fire on both sides our troops had finally yielded to the far superior forces and fled after a loss of nearly five hundred men killed, wounded, and taken prisoner, without loss of any of our officers save for those wounded. Those who escaped joined a party from *Detroit*, part of the *Chevalier de la Corne*'s camp.[101] This same day about two o'clock in the afternoon our generals assembled to deliberate on the plan they would make for the protection of our rapids, in case the enemy, after taking *Niagara,* wanted to take the cavalry post by force, where the *Chevalier de la Corne* is currently camped with one thousand to twelve hundred men, and where our *corvettes* cross. This evening our generals sent out several pickets of regular and Colony troops, five to six hundred Canadians and a few Indians, under the pretext of joining *Mr de Bougainville*, where they were said to fear an attack, wanting to keep the capture of *Niagara* from the public, and the departure of the *Chevalier de Lévis*, who left in the night with *Mr Mercier*, taking a detachment to the cavalry post, which they must reinforce. All day nothing more than a back-and-forth cannonade happened, the enemy fire at *Pointe de Lévy* was directed on the *château* of *Mr le Général*, which is severely hit.

The 12th of August – At three o'clock in the morning, with the winds to the north-east, three-quarter flood tide. One of our guard boats in the harbor signaled the parish village that a group of ships was trying to pass in front of the city. Seeing them, they [the village batteries] began to fire on the most advanced *goélette* which suffered heavy fire all along its route to *l'Anse des Mères*; the three other vessels did not wish to take the risk, returning to anchor among their fleet. This morning at nine o'clock *Mr Reboul* commanded four *jacobite bâteaux* going to attack the *goélette* which had passed in the night, which, after fighting for nearly an hour, was forced to set sail and run aground on the south coast for repairs.[102]

The 13th of August – The enemy's barges seemed to make a lot of movements, which made *Mr de Montcalm* think they would attempt an attack, as a result our

was captured, and died on 28 July of his wounds. C.J. Russ, 'Le Marchand de Lignery, François-Marie', in *Dictionary of Canadian Biography*, vol.3 (Toronto: University of Toronto/Université Laval, 2003–).

101 Chevalier de la Corne, Louis La Corne (Jean-Louis, Pierre, Louis-Luc, Louis-François) Officer of Colonial regular troops. (1703–1761) Identity is often confused due to the variety of ways in which he used in his name. Entered as *enseigne-en-second* in colonial regulars 1722, *enseigne* 1727, *lieutenant* 1738, *capitaine* 1744. In 1759 his weak offensive on the British forces at Oswego helped the British in their advance from the west. C.J. Russ, 'La Corne, Louis de, Chevalier de La Corne', in *Dictionary of Canadian Biography*, vol.3 (Toronto: University of Toronto/Université Laval, 2003–).

102 The journal lists this name as 'Deboulle'. In the *Journal du Siège de Québec* Aegidius Fauteux indicates this name is most likely an error, suggesting it should be *Capitaine* Reboul: Anon., *Journal du Siège de Québec*, (14), p.70. Reboul commanded the merchant ship *St Augustin*, chartered by Cadet as a *munitionnaire*. Couture, '1759: British expedition against Québec'.

army was ordered into the entrenchments, but needlessly. The enemy, after putting on a good show, returned to their different camps from which they fired as usual.

The 14th of August – The enemy encamped at *St Antoine*, where they were said to have been retrenched, set fire to a number of houses in this parish, which they ravaged entirely and drove the beasts to their camp at *Pointe de Lévy*;[103] this day we had four cannon on the ramparts dismounted; nothing remarkable happened at the *Sault*, where there is a lot of firing back and forth.

The 15th of August – Two hours after midday some inhabitants arrived from *Baie St Paul*, who reported that the group of ships in the harbor at *Isle aux Coudres* had made a descent toward them and that, while wanting to oppose it, they had been forced to yield and withdraw into the woods, but the enemy, fearing that there were many people and savages in the woods, returned to their ships after having twenty men killed, the Canadians report. This same day our savages, who had spent two days on the south coast, brought four scalps and two prisoners who report that their generals are beginning to despair of their enterprise. All this day a cannonade was exchanged between the sides.

The 16th of August – Three deserters from the enemy camp at *St Antoine* arrived at the camp of *Mr de Bougainville*, who reported what the prisoners of the city had said, that they are setting fire to all our shores. Indian parties fired on their camp daily, which always killed or wounded some men, that at the camp from which they had deserted there was a lot of talk that *Mr de Bougainville* would attack them shortly, and consequently they worked to entrench themselves. A bomb set fire to two houses in the upper town.

The 17th of August – The enemy continued a lively bombardment on the town, the large number of cannon shots directed on the chateau for several days has put it in risk of imminent collapse. This action greatly inconveniences the *Récollets*, who since the beginning of the bombardment have taken more than two thousand balls and about five hundred bombs, fire-pots and *carcasses* on their ground, which renders it uninhabitable. One of the enemy batteries directed toward the WSW does not treat the Jesuit priests any better, its seminary and the Bishop's house are no more than a stable. In the community only *l'Hôtel Dieu* and the Ursulines have escaped, having so far received only a few bombs and cannonballs, which have not caused much damage to their two houses.[104] This same day the enemy burned about fifteen to twenty houses between *Isle d'Orléans* and *Pointe de Lévy*. Both sides were quiet at the *Sault*.

103 *St Antoine*: on the south bank of the Rivière St Laurent, opposite Jacques Cartier.

104 *Hôtel Dieu*: established at Sillery in 1640 by the canonesses of St Augustine of the Mercy of Jesus, intended to serve the needs of the First Nations people. Moved into the north-east part of Québec City in 1644 due

The 18th of August – At the *Sault* the enemy appeared to embark some pieces of artillery with all the equipment, which makes us believe that they want to leave this area where they already set fire to all the houses on this coast. All day the enemy before the town directed their bombs partly on the clerk's tents, encamped along the *Côte d'Abraham*; partly at the mill on the crossing, where they believe we store powder; and partly at the two vessels anchored at the entrance of the *Rivière St Charles*, without causing any damage; some bombs nearly reached the *Hôpital-Général*,[105] where all the religious of the Ursulines and the *Hôtel Dieu* had taken refuge during the bombardment, and thus a large proportion of the religious women of the city, who deserve the praises of our generals and all the public for their noble offering of succor to all; the *Marquis de Montcalm* has often testified as to his gratitude and proposed to sing their praises to the Court.

The 19th of August – The enemy in front of the city continued their cannonade, for several days they diminished their number of bombs and no longer shoot fire-pots or *carcasses*. They continue to burn the houses in this part [of the city]. This same day at ten o'clock in the evening, after having heard a great deal of cannonfire, a message arrived from *Mr de Bougainville* by which our generals learned that the enemy appeared intent on making a landing below *Pointe aux Trembles*, where their barges sometimes appear to descend, sometimes go up.

The 20th of August – Two hours after midday came a second message which related the enemy had landed at *Deschambault*.[106] *Mr le Marquis de Montcalm* immediately left with our grenadier companies to take command of *Monsieur de Bougainville*'s detachment, who had marched as soon as he saw the enemy disembarked at *Deschambault*; a cavalry squad commanded by *Mr de la Roche*,[107, 108] the

to repeated attacks by the Iroquois. 1693 l'*Hôpital-Général de Québec* opened by Bishop Jean-Baptiste de Saint-Vallier to serve the poor. 1698 the two hospitals merged under the control of the canonesses. See 'Hôtel-Dieu de Québec,' *Wikipedia*.

105 *L'Hôpital-Général*: the General Hospital was located north-west of the city and above the Plains of Abraham, next to an oxbow in the St Charles River and the boat-bridge crossing, outside the range of most British artillery.

106 *Deschambault*: 13 leagues south-west of Québec City on the shore of the Rivière St Laurent.

107 Two light cavalry companies formed of 200 Canadian volunteers under five French officers, formed on 20 June 1759 as scouts and dispatch riders. The French officers were: Louis-Jaçques Ruelle de Santerre, *capitaine*, Languedoc; Pierre Caron Lacourse, *brigadier*, La Marine; Claude Delbreil, *lieutenant*, Béarn; Jean Destrac, *sous-lieutenant*, Béarn; La Roche-Beaucourt, *capitaine*. See below, Government of Canada, 'Database of the 1759–1760 soldiers'.

108 La Roche-Beaucourt (?–1768) cavalry *capitaine* from Saint-Chamond, Loire, France. Government of Canada, 'Database of the 1759–1760 soldiers'. 'The Quebec Volunteer Cavalry, numbering 200 men, were commanded by one of Montcalm's aides-de-camp, a cavalry officer, Capt. La Roche Beaucourt. In patrolling the heights of Sillery during the summer of 1759, clothed in blue and mounted, say Knox, "on neat light horses of different colours," they had from the fleet, quite a picturesque aspect.' Sir James

first to arrive, were no sooner discovered than the enemy turned to re-embark after having burned three houses which contained the baggage of the regular troops, guarded by fifteen invalids commanded by the *Chevalier Perrault*.[109] Having seen the enemy land he had gained a little height with the fifteen invalids, from which he could only watch the burning of his effects and those of his comrades; when *Mr de Bougainville* arrived the enemy were re-embarked with a great quantity of cattle. Our horsemen shot on the rear guard, from which they took three prisoners who stated that one of our inhabitants of *Lotbinière* parish had told them the troop placements and acted as guide for a sum of twenty guineas, that the same inhabitant led them all over the south where he pointed out the *caches* of inhabitants and the hiding places of women in the woods; this fire costs *Père Gabriel* a trunk which was a great loss for a *Récollet*, as it held all his books. At midnight, when the *Marquis de Montcalm* arrived at *Pointe aux Trembles*, he received a message from *Mr de Bougainville* informing him of the re-embarkation of the enemy and the loss of the baggage which he regretted, especially as he had given orders five or six days earlier for it to be taken to *Trois Rivières*. Tonight between nine and ten o'clock a deserter came in from the enemy camp at the *Sault*, who stated that the day before Admiral Saunders had urged General Wolfe to press his expedition,[110] that consequently there had been a great war council in which it had been decided to evacuate the *Sault*, and that since this morning he began to re-embark their artillery. There was some semblance of truth in the testimony of the deserter, our officers of the guard at the entrenchments reported having seen the artillery carted and all day our gunners had aimed their bombs on the barges which crossed to *Isle d'Orléans*; in return they [the British] fired heavily on the city.

The 21st of August – A light back-and-forth bombardment, at the *Sault* the enemy continued to burn the rest of the houses, but they preserved the churches, as they

MacPherson Le Moine, *Quebec, Past and Present: A History of Quebec, 1608-1876*, Volume 2 (Québec: Augustin Coté & Co., 1876), p.143.

109 In his *Journal du Siège de Québec* Aegidius Fauteux indicates that a M. Perrault was the militia captain in charge at Deschambault: Anon., *Journal du Siège de Québec,* (303) p.103 On p.57 of the same text the anonymous journalist indicates the building that was burned belonged to 'Sieur Perault'. Paul Perrault (Perrot, Perreault) (1725–1765) Adjutant General of militia in Canada, farmer as well as involved in trade and transportation. Coordinated men from Deschambault for 1755 advance on Lake Champlain. Malcolm MacLeod, 'Perrault, Paul,' in *Dictionary of Canadian Biography*, vol.3 (Toronto: University of Toronto/Université Laval, 2003–).

110 Sir Charles Saunders (1715–1775) naval officer and office-holder. Entered Royal Navy 1727, 1st lieutenant 1739 aboard the *Centurion* during the 1740–44 circumnavigation of the world. He returned a post-captain, commanding several ships during the Austrian War of Succession. 1749 began his political career while on half-pay during peacetime. 1752 returned to active sea duty while continuing to hold his seat in Parliament. Promoted to rear admiral 1756, 1759 appointed commander of the fleet bound for the Rivière St Laurent. William H. Whiteley, 'Saunders, Sir Charles', in *Dictionary of Canadian Biography*, vol.4 (Toronto: University of Toronto/Université Laval, 2003–).

did at *Isle d'Orléans* and with those on the southern coast, where they appeared to go through several movements of their troops, who ascended to *la Rivière des Etchemins* above *Sault de la Chaudière.*

The 22nd of August – The fire of the batteries on all sides was its slowest, especially at the *Sault* where the enemy continued to re-embark their artillery, which two deserters who arrived this afternoon assured.

The 23rd of August – One of our savages arrived after an absence of ten or twelve days, during which he was thought to have been killed when, being alone, he passed the crossing at *Sault Montmorency*, ignoring our sentinels, saying that he wished to take a scalp in the enemy's entrenchments. Finding them dead at its bottom, he fell asleep. The enemy did not see him until later, a guard came to surround him just as he woke. Our savage was surprised to be taken to General Wolfe, who had his hands and feet shackled and had him led through the camp, after which he was sent on board the flagship, where after a few days our savage learned to keep out of sight, decided to swim to safety and thus on the night of the 23rd to the 24th was able to shed his irons and tricked the sentinels, threw his blanket over the ship's starboard side while he slipped to the port. The ruse worked. The enemy immediately believed the blanket in the water was him and shot at it. Some sailors gave chase in a boat but to their surprise found only a blanket while our savage gained the south coast, who after drawing a few shots from the camp guards without injury, he slipped into the woods and mocked his enemies. All day heavy cannon shots fell on the city while the enemy's *Sault* camp remained tranquil.

The 24th of August – After several requests from the Canadian residents to return home, they again solicited the *Général* to allow them to go to harvest, which the *Général* refused, promising to provide for them. But the Canadians did not seem to want to rely on the promises of the *Général*, all but 200 leaving by night without the *Général*'s orders, despite the complaints of the *Marquis de Montcalm*, who fears the enemy's interpretation of this desertion, which he estimates at more than two thousand men; ordinary cannon fire on both sides.

The 25th of August – A *goélette* and several of our *bâteaux* laden with food from *Jacques Cartier* were seen by the enemy who detached a frigate and several *bâteaux* to intercept our boats, which had time to enter the river at *Cap Rouge* where our men, after landing, waited with feet firm: the frigate, after some cannon shots, withdrew to the barges, and the barges went back to join their ships; all this day passed without any movement on the part of the enemy who continued to bombard the city.

The 26th of August – Nothing remarkable happened in the different enemy camps, who for several days have not been able to fire any more from the *Sault*. They continued to have a great deal of effect on the *Isle d'Orléans* and *Pointe de Lévy* from which they fired very little this day.

The 27th of August – It was ordered by our generals to gather all the sailors scattered on the batteries to arm five of our frigates, the *Marchault*, the *Chézine*, the *Maréchal Senneterre*, the *Manon*, and the *Bienfaisant* to bring them down to *Pointe aux Trembles*, where they must fight against the enemy ships.[111] Accordingly seven marine officers attached to the ammunition service received orders to leave the next night, all things being arranged. Our officers left around nine o'clock in the evening to *Petite Rivière*, to meet six or seven hundred sailors, and from there pass on the road where they were seen by the enemy and were heavily bombarded. They continued on their way to *Pointe aux Trembles* where they received another bombardment from the vessels, but without any losses. Finally they happily returned to *Cap Santé*, where our frigates divided them among the ships, awaiting the orders of the *Général*; all day the enemy heavily bombarded the city.

The 28th of August – With north-east winds the enemy took advantage of the evening tide to pass four ships in the darkness of night which, despite the sharp fire from our ramparts, joined their ships at *Pointe aux Trembles*, which led our generals to send orders to the officers of the frigates not to descend, to continue to occupy the *Richelieu* harbor, and to send back the sailors, who regretted losing the opportunity to act. Normal cannonfire on the city all day.

The 29th of August – Our sailors arrived with provisions for the army. As soon as they were disembarked they were all to take possession of the posts they previously held, with orders to keep a good guard, as a result of the statement made by a deserter that morning who reported that the enemy planned to anchor four warships broadside in front of the city and try a landing there, at the same time they try one at *Pointe aux Trembles*, but the *Marquis de Montcalm* gave his orders in vain, the enemy did nothing else but to bombard the city.

The 30th of August – The enemy at the *Sault* burned the rest of their entrenchments and seemed to raise a camp on *Isle d'Orléans*, at the same place which they occupied previously, that they were not slow to evacuate the *Sault* and take possession of this new camp; from *Pointe de Lévy* the enemy continued to fire actively on the city.

111 *Le Marchault* out of Bordeaux, 500–550 tons. Jacques Cannon, *capitaine*. *Proprio*: Pierre Desclaux & *Fils aîné*. *L'Aimable Manon*, 400 tons. Martin Minbielle, *capitaine*. *Proprio*: Pierre Desclaux. *Le Bienfaisant* out of Bordeaux, 340–350 tons. François Courval, *capitaine*. *Proprio*: La Malétie et La Tuilière. Campeau, *Navires Venus en Nouvelle-France*.

The 31st of August – The enemy, after setting fire to their works at the *Sault*, embarked and were encamped at *Isle d'Orléans*, part at *Pointe de Lévy* where their camp appeared most considerable, and where they made great movements of their troops, having them sometimes embark, sometimes pass in front of the city, appearing in front of it for a long time arranged in battle lines. Finally they sent it up to the *Rivière Etchemins*, where it plunges into the wilderness, and remained all night under arms. All that day there was bombarding on both sides. The same day the *Marquis de Montcalm*, after the enemy had evacuated the *Sault*, moved our camp. He ordered the *Montréal* militia from the *Sault* camp to come and camp with the *Québec* militia at *La Canardière*, and the *Guyenne* regiment to come camp to the right of the bridge at the crossing, to be able to cross the fields there, preventing the enemy from making further attempts, leaving the *Royal Roussillon* regiment at the works at the *Sault*, with six to seven hundred men of the militia. All things being so disposed our *Général* came to occupy the center of the army, making his headquarters. All day the city sent a quantity of bombs on the enemy batteries which replied with a large number of cannon rounds.

The 1st of September – At the evening tide and in north-easterly winds, the enemy in front of the city fired briskly in order to facilitate the passage of several of their ships wanting to join those anchored at *Cap Rouge*, despite the heavy fire from our ramparts above, from which our cannon could do no damage.

The 2nd of September – As the winds continued fresh from north-east, it was feared that the enemy would send other ships to join the 17 presently above the town. In consequence the *Général* ordered a careful guard of the city and the harbor. The *Marquis de Montcalm* ordered the *Guyenne* regiment to leave one hour before sunrise each day, and to post under the walls of the city, prepared for immediate movement wherever there is need or the enemy might appear and try to advance: *Mr de Bougainville*, with three companies of grenadiers and about twelve hundred men, guards the coast from *Cap Rouge* to *Pointe aux Trembles*. Ordinary cannonade on the city.

The 3rd of September – *Mr de Repentigny*, with about seven hundred men, passed the Sault where he distributed his men to guard this coast as far as *St Joachim*, to let the inhabitants take in their harvest, which the enemy have not damaged.[112] This precaution by our generals is in consequence of two enemy vessels which had anchored at *l'Ange Gardien* crossing. This same day the enemy continued to ravage the coasts of *Isle d'Orléans* and *Pointe de Lévy*, where they continued to bombard the city and put it in a sorry state.

112 *St Joachim*: above the NE tip of the Isle d'Orléans and NE of Beaupré.

The 4th of September – The enemy opened a new battery of five guns in the intervals, protecting the mortars with an embankment three feet high, a target for our artillerymen with little chance of dismounting them. For nearly two months the enemy have extended from one side of the city to the other. The city could not be in a more pitiable state unless it is razed.

The 5th of September – At daybreak the enemy appeared, during vessel maneuvers, to make considerable movements with their barges as if they wished to try a descent at *La Canardière*, calling our army into the entrenchments, but unnecessarily as they [the enemy] returned to *Pointe de Lévy*, from which they continue to bombard the city. This same day our savages from the south coast brought four scalps and two prisoners who state that Mr General Wolfe exercises his troop daily for a next descent.

The 6th of September – The ships made different movements in the fleet and an enemy force of three or four thousand men appeared several times at the edge of the woods opposite the city, who finally marched to *Sault de la Chaudière*, where they raised a camp;[113] a great cannonade on the city this day.

The 7th of September – At three o'clock in the afternoon the enemy sent a twelve-ton *goélette* which, receiving heavy fire from our ramparts, went up and joined the vessels above the town. The balls fired from *Pointe de Lévy* killed an officer and two sailors; this day many of our *carcassières* were aimed at a frigate at *Cap Rouge*, with no other harm than both sides having been bombarded for more than an hour.

The 8th of September – About sixty barges were seen leaving *Pointe de Lévy*, which after several movements ranged under *Beauport* feigning a descent, but we had not fired half a dozen cannon shots from one of our redoubts when the enemy returned to their camp at *Pointe de Lévy*, from which the fire of their batteries was its slowest; they behave differently in ravaging our coasts, where all is fire and blood; this same day, despite the heavy fire from our ramparts, the enemy took advantage of the morning tide and the north-east winds, passing four of their vessels to join those anchored at *Pointe aux Trembles*.

The 9th of September – There was nothing remarkable. The enemy fire on the city consisted of about twenty cannon shots, many movements which resulted in giving exercise to our army, who have been sleeping at arms nightly for the last two months.

113 *Sault de la Chaudière*: south of the Rivière St Laurent and south-west of Québec City.

The 10th of September – Some inhabitants of the southern coast reported to our generals that thirty vessels descended the river, and that there were great troop movements daily at *Pointe de Lévy*; despite the heavy rains this day the enemy maintained a lively bombardment of the city on which they also threw some bombs.

The 11th of September – A barge sounded the channel above the *Pointe à Carcy*, where the enemy threw several balls.[114] *Mr Le Gris* was cut down by the heavy fire of a frigate which advanced on him; the enemy fired onto the city accomplishing little.

The 12th of September – At seven o'clock in the evening the enemy, after a great cannonade all day long, made a number of signals to which the vessels above and below the city responded all night, and there were great movements among their vessels; our generals note the vigilance of *Mr de Bougainville* who continues to observe the enemy from *St Augustin* to *Pointe aux Trembles*, where the other two grenadier companies have been for a few days.[115]

The 13th of September – After big movements the day before, the enemy left in the night from *l'Anse au Foulon* for *Pointe aux Trembles*, where they drew *Mr de Bougainville* with all his troops, pretending to finally have resolved to attempt a landing at the said place, where the barges came lying to until two o'clock at night. They benefited from the falling tide and the fresh south-west winds to descend and anchor their vessels at *Samos*, where having arrived, two frigates and two *bâteaux* left and came to anchor across from *l'Anse Foulon*, the post where *Mr Vergor* was stationed for three or four days with sixty men,[116] a simple precaution on the part

114 *Pointe à Carcy*: north of Québec City, at the mouth of the St Charles River.

115 *St Augustin*: SW of the *Cap Rouge* River on the northern shore of the Rivière St Laurent.

116 *Capitaine* Louis Dupont de Chambon de Vergor (1713–1775) Compagnies franches de la marine, commanding the picquet that night. In his pension application, Vergor described the events: 'In 1759 during the siege of Quebec, he [Vergor] was ordered on 2 September by the general to go and relieve the S[ieu]r. de St. Martin at his post at the Foulon Cove where he and 70 men were stationed. On the 12th [of September], he received an order to allow the passage of a convoy of boats that were to go down [the river] during the night of the 12th to 13th, to take provisions to Quebec, and he gave orders accordingly and had the sentries warned to allow the vessels in question to pass through, after, however, having recognized [identified] them. 3 hours before daybreak, the sentries gave notice that the vessels were in sight and they immediately demanded "where the boats had come from, from which regiment, and where they were going," to which they [the boats] replied "France. Marine" and that "they were on their way to Quebec with provisions." Continuing to observe these boats, which had already passed by their post, the sentries noticed that they were coming round and trying to enter the Cove and assumed that they were the enemy and did not hesitate a moment to make arrangements to fire upon them. At the same time, a man of his detachment was sent to his camp to warn that the post was about to be attacked and that the enemy were attempting to land in the cove. It was two hours after midnight. They did their utmost to prevent the enemy coming ashore, with the intention of delaying, to give time for help to arrive, and the

of our generals anticipating the enemy would wish to take this post, which they regarded as impossible in the steepest coastal location, where a man alone had difficulty in ascending, was nevertheless the site the enemy chose for their landing; from their battery in front of the town they had no sooner seen the frigates than they began their largest bombardment on the city, where two barges loaded with about forty men, Brigadier Murray in the lead, left their ships and landed right near *l'Anse au Foulon*, and being seen by one of *Mr Vergor*'s guards, who asked 'Who goes?', immediately a man from the barges speaking good French replied '*France*', enjoining the guard not to make any noise, as he was to spend the night on our *bâteaux* laden with food. The guard thought it was our people trying to pass, shouted to the barges to proceed, which after going higher, the officer landed his troops with a great deal of caution and climbed the coast with considerable difficulty. Reaching the top he found no resistance and made a signal calling other barges to leave the ships to join them. Mr General Wolfe took the front with only sixty men and during the landing our guard, seeing that the enemy were at his post, flew to his camp. Mr Murray immediately advanced with his thirty men instead of Mr Wolfe having to climb with the sixty men who were not yet on the top of the shore. They rushed *Mr Vergor*'s guard, who stood with thirty men and after a slight resistance fled when they saw *Mr Vergor* wounded; having realized that the enemy were taking control of *Mr Vergor*'s post, the city signaled to warn the *Guyenne* regiment's camp immediately, which for several days had not marched below the city. Leaving the camp to meet the enemy, they found 1,500 men already ranged in battle lines atop a rise. The *Guyenne* regiment with three to four hundred Canadians realized the impossibility of preventing the enemy from fully making their landing, took the left and formed in battle lines half a rifle's shot from the enemy column. Meanwhile the orders of the *Marquis de Montcalm* who, when the city had signaled, was being ordered by the *Général* to take the reserve army which had been held for the defense of the entrenchments, to join the field of battle without delay, where he spent between seven and eight hours at the head of the battalions of *La Sarre*, *Languedoc* and *Béarn*, finding seven to eight thousand enemy troops in three columns which were entrenching. Their first column, five or

enemy was thus held back until daylight arrived when, finding themselves turned and outflanked everywhere by different pickets [detachments] that the enemy had sent down to St. Michel and Samos, they were finally overpowered. The greater part of his force was killed or wounded, and this moreover was not until after having himself been twice wounded, once by a ball that which broke his leg, and the other in his hand. The enemy succeeded in forcing his post and climbing up [the heights] above the shore. Taken on the battlefield, he [Vergor] was put aboard a sloop, where he found himself with 14 English officers who had been wounded in this action; another sloop was entirely filled with their wounded soldiers.' Donald E. Graves, 'The Anse au Foulon, 1759: Some New Theories and Some New Evidence', *The Northern Mariner* 14:4(October 2004), https://www.cnrs-scrn.org/northern_mariner/vol14/tnm_14_4_61-72.pdf (accessed 3 September 2018), p.69; and Bernard Pothier, 'Dupont de Chambon de Vergor, Louis', in *Dictionary of Canadian Biography*, vol.4 (Toronto: University of Toronto/Université Laval, 2003–).

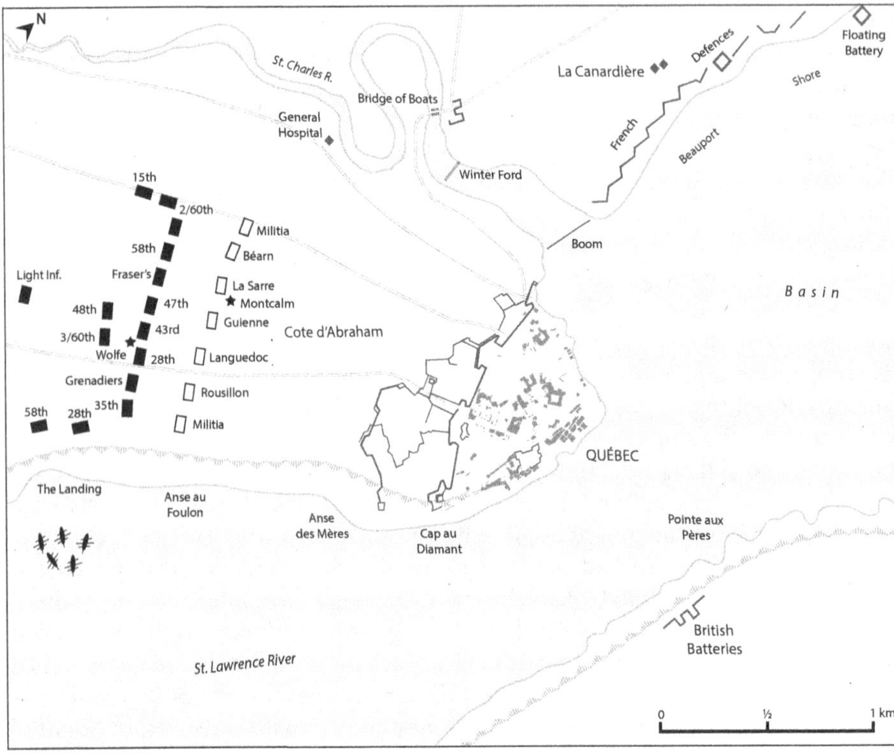

Map 4 Battle of the Plains of Abraham, 13 September 1759.

six in depth, ranged from the landing place to the *Borgia* house, or in [blank space] 3 to 4 hundred men were entrenched, the second [column] was formed with two six-pound guns. Finally the third supported their first two along the *St Foi* road, against the arrival of *Mr Bougainville* who was seen to be on the way. The *Marquis de Montcalm* not recognizing the strengths and the advantageous situation of the enemy, who occupied the height, ordered that five guns of twelve, six and four pounds were brought, with powder and balls. The *Marquis'* orders were executed promptly, the cannon arrived, two were placed to the left of our column, on the side of the *Porte St Louis*, one in the center looking down *St Foi* Road, and one on the right along the *Côte d'Abraham*. As the rest of the troops arrived they were put in battle order and were commanded by the *Marquis de Montcalm*, who had seven or eight hundred Canadians and Indians placed on the flanks of our column, who, by their fire and the fire which they set at the *Borgia* house, toward nine, fought the fiercest of the action, which *Mr de Montcalm* thought it best to maintain, and to profit by the advance of our column, as soon as the troops seemed best disposed, to the bottom of the height occupied by the enemy, within range. The enemy stood firm through three discharges of our column, descended almost within reach;

never was action more obstinate when, after nearly half an hour, *Monsieur de Montcalm* was wounded and our men felt all was lost. They immediately abandoned the field of battle to the enemy, who pressed their advantage and pursued our army to just below the walls of the city, while part of our right column was pursued into *Mr Flichet*'s fields, a sad spectacle for those who watched from the windows of the General Hospital. Never would I have imagined that the loss of a general could cause a defeat, I dare say without example. On the plain, only the *Marquis de Vaudreuil* could succeed in rallying our troops to turn against the enemy who pursued them, no one doubting that a panic seized our people who were also cowardly. They had been brave at the beginning of the action, but *Montcalm* was no longer there and the brave men were gone, the fatal day which changed the colony. An irreparable day that cost the life of the conqueror at *Chouaguin* [Oswego], Fort George, and *Carillon*, where with three thousand men he beat from seventeen to eighteen thousand of the enemy. Wishing to God that he had heard of the arrival of *Mr Bougainville*, who had all the grenadier companies, pickets, volunteers, and elite militia, totaling two thousand men, who joined with the three thousand five hundred already at the battle, and would have hurt the enemy, in the judgment of anyone, not an Englishman would re-embark. But unfortunately *Mr de Montcalm* let it fall to a troop which he foresaw he could no longer hold back, as soon as the Canadians and the Indians on the right and the left flanks were overrun with enemies. This is the end of the famous battle of the 13th day, in which the enemy of their own admission had more than four hundred men killed and about two hundred wounded, General Wolfe killed and the two near him wounded, our loss totals one hundred and fifty men killed and nearly three hundred wounded. The enemy have completely abandoned the height and forced our army to enter the entrenchments back on the battlefield, where they began to build batteries and uselessly continued to entrench. In the afternoon several Canadians and marines tried to provide covering fire to encourage our people to remove our wounded, but they were forced to withdraw, the enemy having advanced to the edge of a scrub, and after having posted guards they themselves removed what wounded were left on both sides. As soon as the *Marquis de Montcalm* was wounded, he was sent into the city where the surgeons, after inspecting the wound, decided that he did not have twenty-four hours to live, the *Marquis* distraught thinking his army cut to pieces, an idea disabused before he died. During the battle and all the rest of the day the city fired more fiercely on the [British] barges and *chaloupes* laden with war goods and provisions from *Pointe de Lévy* to the battlefield, but the city's wish to resist is in vain, reduced since the bombing into a state not to see, or to lodge, unsheltered, with no hope, no assistance from our army which in the night fell back to *St Augustin* after abandoning war goods and provisions as well as equipment in the trenches, items for looting by the savages and inhabitants. Only a cavalry officer with one hundred and thirty men remained in the entrenchments to watch the enemy who, in the night, cut off the front of the passage, took the powder, spiked the cannons, and set the floating battery on fire. It was unfortunate that at the departure of our army Mr Bigot had neglected to instruct M. de Ramezay, who commanded the city, to gather provisions that had been abandoned in the camp, which would have supplied M. de Ramezay for some time, while waiting for the *Chevalier de Lévis*, for whom a courier had been sent, asking him to come and take the command of the wreckage of the army, and who possibly would go and take revenge for the thirteenth and our army. But the death of the *Marquis de Montcalm*, having come during the night, made me lose my belief in those on whom command rested, who were fleeing, so much did they fear that the enemy would try to force our entrenchments the next day.

During the night from the 13th to the 14th the enemy made a great movement. They were able to scout the passage after having reached the suburbs of *St Roche*, and finally they came at midnight to the General Hospital where all the injured were, where according to the agreement they posted a safeguard. They posted another guard at the mill which covered the passage on the road to *Petite Rivière*. A third guard was posted at the mill above the *Côte d'Abraham*, where they established a redoubt, in which they had two pieces of cannon which fired at night on the two vessels anchored at *Petite Rivière*.

The 14th of September – The enemy approached the walls of the city within range, where they opened a trench; city opposition is in vain as they establish batteries which will take aim on the *St Louis* bastion. This is not a feint to hide their intentions to climb our walls, for the defense of which there remain about fifteen hundred men of which more than a third are Canadians, of whom the [blank space] and fear makes you flee to join our army that is said to be camped from *Pointe aux Trembles* to *Cap Rouge*, after having abandoned the entrenchments with an unparalleled disorder. This same day the enemy came to the bridge, but our people who in the night had placed three or four cannon in case they were attacked, defended it so firmly that the enemy were forced to retreat behind the parapets of the mill where, after having removed a large quantity of powder which they found in the public house, and looted the goods belonging to private persons of the city, set fire to the house, then returned to the entrance of the suburb of *St Roche* whence their soldiers were seen carrying away a quantity of effects. At eight o'clock at night, in the Ursuline Church, the *Marquis de Montcalm* was buried in a bomb crater, having died at four o'clock in the morning after having received all the Sacraments. Never before had a general been loved more by his troops, and more universally regretted. He was of a superior mind, generous, sweet, affable, familiar to everyone which had gained him the confidence of the whole colony. *Requiescat in pace.*

The 15th of September – The city, which for two days had been invested, made their last vain efforts with a heavy bombarding of the enemy camp: a sad situation for a brave man who finds himself defending a similarly sad place, reduced to two days of food at a quarter ration, with a bit of grains, a ration which he is obliged to decrease as women come for protection, whose number since the day of battle has risen to four thousand, without the hope of help from our army who appear insensitive to the cries of a populace demanding food, and finally to stop listening to representations of the negotiators who told them that it would be expedient for their wellbeing and that of the people to treat with the enemy, to be able to obtain an honorable capitulation, that the enemy could not refuse a defense for more than two months, that in vain we would try to resist more than three days, at which time it would be necessary to surrender without being able to obtain what we were entitled to through capitulation: such was the situation of *Mr de Ramezay*, King's Lieutenant and commander of the city. This same day *Mr le Marquis de Vaudreuil* sent an officer to the English general to beg him to send a list of our officers held prisoner and enjoin him to care for our wounded. This evening *Mr de Ramezay* assembled all the officers of the garrison to deliberate what part they would take in the case they remained more than three days without help from our army. Only the actions of this war council can make known what was decided.

The 16th of September – The enemy sent different detachments to *Cap Rouge* and to the parish of *Lorette* to cut off all communication between our army and the city, and consequently they stopped men, women and children whom they found by the roads and led them to the camp. They were questioned what general had given them permission to enter the town, and not allowed to continue.

The 17th – The city, which could only be served with great difficulty by three cannons and two mortars on the ramparts facing the enemy, nevertheless made a most lively fire on the workers in the trench, which is open in ground so uneven it is hardly visible from our ramparts. By the presence of the English officers who made the walk from their camp to the hospital, it was evident that our balls and bombs did not trouble them and that within three days at the latest they would have a battery of twenty-six to thirty cannon of thirty-six pounds which would batter in short order; all day our detachment at the bridge exchanged fire with the enemy's guard beyond the mill. Our vessels anchored at the entrance of *Rivière St Charles* fired actively on the enemy redoubt established at the top of the *Côte d'Abraham*, whence the enemy fired all day on the palace battery from which our people responded, but all their balls fell short. Toward midday several warships detached from the fleet and anchored at *Pointe de Lévy* leading one to think that they wanted to form a blockade in the night, which gave rise to a heightened watch over the rampart batteries defending the harbor, where two-thirds of the garrison worked in service of the guns. This same evening the different movements of the enemy led *Mr de Ramezay* to believe that they [the British] might have decided to climb the city walls, and being reduced to only one hundred damp packets of provisions that he had just received, with no sign of other aid, he finally thought it necessary to treat for an honorable capitulation and consequently he deputed *Mr*

Joannès, Capitaine Aide-Major of the *Languedoc* regiment,[117] to carry the demands our commander would like to ask of the enemy before giving them this place, to which they consented except that the garrison would not be returned to the army, to which *Mr Joannès* pretended to be unable to agree without the orders of the commander; for this purpose the enemy granted to *Mr Joannès* a delay from seven until eleven o'clock to inform *Mr Ramezay*, who immediately returned *Mr Joannès* with orders to conclude the capitulation. All night the weather was rainy, in the absence of our officer we kept careful guard on the ramparts facing the enemy's camp.

The 18th of September – At eight o'clock in the morning *Mr Joannès* returned with three copies of the capitulation, which *Mr de Ramezay* had signed and kept a copy of it, sending the two others back to the English general, who detached some grenadier companies to take possession of the gates of the city, while waiting for the enemy garrison assigned to take possession of the city, which they effected at half-past three, when it was agreed that it would be six o'clock in the evening of the same day that the capitulation would be signed.

Articles of capitulation requested by Mr de Ramezay, King's Lieutenant commanding the upper and lower city of Québec, Chevalier of the military order of St Louis, to His Excellency the General of His Britannic Majesty's forces	**The capitulation as requested was granted by His Excellency General Townshend, Brigadier of the Army of His Britannic Majesty in the manner and conditions expressed below**
Article 1 Mr de Ramsay asks for the honors of war for the garrison and that they be safely returned to the army by the shortest route, with their arms and baggage, six bronze cannons, two mortars or howitzers, and 12 rounds for each.	*Article 1* The garrison of the city, composed of Colony troops, marines, and sailors will leave the city with arms, luggage, drums beating, linstocks lit, two French cannons, and 12 rounds for each piece, to be transported as commodiously as is possible to the first port in France.
Article 2 That the inhabitants shall retain possession of their homes and privileges.	*Article 2* Agreed, on their laying down their arms.

117 Égide-Armand [Gilles-Armand] Joannès (1735–1814) *lieutenant-en-second* 1747, *lieutenant* 1750, adjutant 1753, *capitaine* 1755, engineer 1757 *capitaine* in Languedoc, served as interpreter for de Ramezay and Brigadier Townshend at the surrender of Québec. Government of Canada, 'Database of the 1759–1760 soldiers'.

Articles of capitulation requested by Mr de Ramezay, King's Lieutenant commanding the upper and lower city of Québec, Chevalier of the military order of St Louis, to His Excellency the General of His Britannic Majesty's forces	**The capitulation as requested was granted by His Excellency General Townshend, Brigadier of the Army of His Britannic Majesty in the manner and conditions expressed below**
Article 3 That said inhabitants shall not be prosecuted for having taken up arms in defense of the city, as they were forced, and that the inhabitants of the two crown colonies served equally as soldiers.	*Article 3* Agreed …
Article 4 They shall not molest the property of the absent officers or citizens.	*Article 4* Agreed …
Article 5 That the inhabitants shall not be moved or required to leave their homes until it is settled between His Most Christian Majesty and His Britannic Majesty, having settled their states.	*Article 5* Agreed …
Article 6 That the practice of the Catholic, Apostolic, and Roman religion shall be continued; that they grant safeguard to ecclesiastical houses and convents, particularly to Monsignor Leveque, Bishop of *Québec*, who is filled with zeal for religion and charity for the people, and his diocese wishes to continue to freely exercise with the decency which his status and the sacred offices of the Roman religion require, his episcopal authority in the city of *Québec*, when it is judged appropriate, until the possession of Canada has been decided between His Most Christian Majesty and His Britannic Majesty.	*Article 6* Free exercise of the Roman religion is granted to all religious persons, and to Mr Leveque, who shall be at liberty to come and exercise, freely and with decency, the functions of his office, whenever he shall think proper, until the possession of Canada is decided between His Most Christian Majesty and His Britannic Majesty.
Article 7 That the artillery and war materials shall be surrendered in good faith, and that an inventory shall be completed.	*Article 7* Agreed …

Articles of capitulation requested by Mr de Ramezay, King's Lieutenant commanding the upper and lower city of Québec, Chevalier of the military order of St Louis, to His Excellency the General of His Britannic Majesty's forces	**The capitulation as requested was granted by His Excellency General Townshend, Brigadier of the Army of His Britannic Majesty in the manner and conditions expressed below**
Article 8 That they will treat the wounded and sick, the commissaries, chaplains, doctors, surgeons, apothecaries, and other people employed in the service hospitals in accordance with the treaty of 6 February 1759 agreed between their Majesties Most Christian and Britannic.	*Article 8* Agreed ...
Article 9 That before surrendering the gate and the entrance of the city to the English troops, their general shall assign several soldiers to safeguard churches, convents churches, and principal habitations.	*Article 9* Agreed ...
Article 10 That the King's Lieutenant commanding the city of *Québec* to send a message to *Mr le Marquis de Vaudreuil*, Governor-General, informing him of the reduction of the place, as also the General may write to the Minister of France to inform him.	*Article 10* Agreed ...
Article 11 That this capitulation will be executed according to its form and tenor without it being subject to non-execution under pretense of reprisals, or for non-execution of any previous capitulations.	*Article 11* [Agreed ...]

The above treaty was executed in duplicate between us, at the camp before *Québec*, the 18th of September, 1759. Signed now by Saunders, De Ramezay, Townshend.

The 19th of September – The enemy, despite the garrison which they had sent to occupy the city center, placed an additional body of 4 to 500 troops, their artillery which had battered the place, a quantity of munitions and provisions; ships entered the harbor and anchored in two lines from *l'Anse de Sillery* to *Sault Montmorency*; they landed a body of 1,200 to 1,300 men who were encamped on the *Côte d'Abraham* where they had driven a quantity of oxen, cows, and sheep. This same day our detachment at the bridge, despite the relinquishment of the place, wished to continue to defend it, firing actively on the various enemy detachments which went beyond it. The English general sent one of his officers to *Mr de Ramezay* to inform him that he had to remove the troops from the bridge and bring them under the guns of the city. *Mr de St Vincent* was sent to enjoin our officer to withdraw, which having accomplished, the enemy immediately seized our entrenchments, from which they took what munitions and provisions they found, and pillaged the remaining equipment of our army. Two officers detached from the *Général* arrived though nothing is known about their embassy. This day the garrison embarked.

The 20th of September – Several deserters from our army arrived at the city who by their depositions, though unknown to us, caused great movements to be made by the enemy, who ascended with a great number of barges to *Cap Rouge*, where the day before they sent a detachment of five or six hundred men to occupy this post, and a similar number to *Lorette* to cut off all communication to our army. One could no longer travel without a passport from an English general, no longer leave the city. However, during the night, a number of soldiers, sailors, and Canadians would escape to join our army, which the enemy perceived and fired grapeshot on them; in spite of this precaution on their part, our troops continued to escape when they saw an opportunity.

The 21st of September – The townsmen and inhabitants outlying *Québec*, three leagues round, took the oath of fidelity, a ceremony which lasted from the morning until about three o'clock in the afternoon, when the English general made a declaration by which it was permitted to go and come freely, to go about their business and to remain the owners of their property, but what good does it do for our people to go to occupy what they have ravaged, burned houses, stolen beasts, and plundered furniture? This day we saw our poor women come out from the depths of the woods, dragging after them their little children, eaten by flies without clothes, crying with hunger. What a wounding of the poor mothers, who do not know if they have husbands, and where they were taken, and how will they sustain their poor children at the start of a season during which it is difficult to protect themselves. When they are arranged in their households the sieges of Jerusalem and Samarie are no more dreadful.

The 22nd of September – Admiral Saunders sent word to *Mr de Ramezay* and the officers of the garrison, and to all those who were going to France to board their ships. *Mr de Ramezay*, whom I was to see at about six o'clock in the morning, told me to embark with *Mr de St Vincent*, captain of the colony, *Chevalier de St Louis*, on the ship *Le Haupoint* which was already loaded with 68 sailors of my battery, at nine o'clock, after having bid farewell to the gentlemen of the Seminary with whom I boarded during the siege, I embarked.[118]

118 *Le Haupoint*: in the 23 September entry he lists his ship as the Honfwot. I find no such named ships listed as having been active in Québec at this time, either English or French.

The 23rd of September – At about ten o'clock in the morning we sailed four [*sic*] packet-boats, the *Aid Marie*, the *Lauret*, the *Honfwot* on which I am with about 280 sailors. At ten o'clock we sailed in ENE winds, almost calm. The weather hazy when two *chaloupes* from beside the flagship came to tow us. Toward midday the winds having freshened WNW we put out all the sails and continued our route to the front of the fleet, where we arrived at six o'clock in the evening and were obliged to drop anchor across from the end of *Isle d'Orléans*, 7 leagues from *Québec*.

The 24th of September – At 7 o'clock in the morning the winds continued fresh WNW, variable to WSW. We sailed from the harbor of *Isle Madame*, where we left 13 enemy warships anchored between three others of three bridges, and two frigates or *corvettes*. A 30-gun frigate with us from the *Québec* harbor is expected to convoy us beyond the river. We followed this set route to find the channel, having the *Amare* to port heading from NE to N. At midday we were near the crossing at *St Anne*. We followed our route to the *Isle aux Coudres*, heading at ENE and NE 1/4 E. At 2 o'clock in the afternoon we reached *Isle aux Coudres*, where we found 8 ships, 2 frigates and a bomb *galliote* anchored in this bay. Following our route at full sail, travelling ENE by E 1/4 SE to pick up the Pellerins, where we anchored at 6 o'clock in the evening in 16 fathoms of water, sandy muddy bottom, 25 to 30 leagues from *Québec*.

Tuesday the 25th of September – At 6 o'clock in the morning we had raised anchor, full sails out, big fresh winds from WNW, clear weather heading NE and NE 1/4 E until six o'clock at night. We dropped anchor at *Isle au Lièvre* (Hare Island) in the west of *Pot de l'Eau de Vie*, in 8 fathoms of water, a bottom of fine sand and mud, 35 to 40 leagues from *Québec*.

The 26th of September – The winds at WNW were fresh, the day clear and cold. We were very surprised in the morning not to set sail, only then our captain told us that the frigate that conveyed us was remaining to guard us until the arrival of Admiral Durell, who sails out with us from the river.[119] Despite representations that *Mr de Ramezay* sent the captain of the frigate, who gave no more response than to say that such were his orders, he did not take the trouble each day to notice the favorable WSW wind and their ship had to wait and exercise patience. A sad fate to be seen on a poor ship, [the passengers] piled on top of each other without any other food than fully rotten biscuits or some kind of oatmeal, there

119 Philip Durell (1707–1766) British naval officer, second in command of the fleet at the Siege of Québec in 1759. Entered the navy as an ordinary seaman 1721, able seaman 1724, lieutenant 1731, captain 1742. A surveyor, he provided detailed plans for Louisbourg harbor in 1745. Commodore January 1758, rear admiral July 1758. W.A.B. Douglas, 'Durell, Philip,' in *Dictionary of Canadian Biography*, vol.3 (Toronto: University of Toronto/Université Laval, 2003–).

is half-straw to be boiled with a little bit of tallow. This is the food that we were given Monday, Wednesday, Friday. Sunday, Tuesday and Thursday we were given rotten salted beef or pretty good bacon. Finally Saturday we are given some green peas and butter and a little bit of cheese. It is thus that we are treated and that we will be treated until our arrival in *France*, we have no other expectation. Our fear is that disease is kept from the ship, the ills have already started to thin us. We other marine officers are fortunate in that *Mr de St Vincent* is embarked with his family, well-provided with provisions that he absolutely wants to share with us. He is most obliging to act amiably with us, sharing amusing stories, easing our existence. We waited 20 days without Admiral Durell having appeared to want to come, which determined *Mr de Ramezay* to dispatch *Mr de Joannès* to the admiral to see what he planned to do with us, and that he was surprised after the firm promises he had received, to send him to France with his garrison most conveniently and by the shortest way, he risked exposing all the garrison to death; it is unknown whether this representation took place or that Admiral Durell departed at this time, but he appeared on the 19th of October at daybreak, and when he was through us he signaled to sail. Our sailors willingly lent their hands at this moment to raise the anchor and set sail, about 11 o'clock; the winds turned against us toward 4 o'clock in the evening, to NE, but the wind fell flat at 6 o'clock. We dropped anchor below the isle of Bic, in 13 fathoms of water, bottom of sand and gravel. The next day, after the Admiral had sent us water, biscuits and bacon to replace that which we have consumed since our departure from *Québec* aboard our four packet-boats, he signaled to sail, which we did joyously for over 11 hours.

The 20th of October – Variable winds from SSW to west a little fresh and fine weather, heading east and E 1/4 SE, at full sail. At 4 o'clock the winds became contrary from the SSE. We were becalmed for nearly two days before the winds blew SE for 6 or 7 hours, then came a great WNW wind. We took all the reefs with topsails and maintained at ESE, overcast and rainy weather continuing up to the Grand Bank of Newfoundland, where we fought contrary SE winds for about 10 hours, lightly fresh, then the winds reversed WSW variable to WNW with clear weather and finally beautiful seas carrying full sail, and keeping the route at SE 1/4 E and ESE which pushed us to far below the Azores isles, where after a day of calm they came back to SW great and fresh, which pushed us *en route* to the prime meridian on the 8th of November. At four o'clock in the evening we found a small Guernsey corsair of 12 guns who after having asked for news of their army from *Québec*, tells us that it was 160 leagues from Cape Lizard in 14 days, he [the captain of the corsair] was English and that he had not learned of the fall of *Québec* before his departure, so that for proof of rejoicing he shouted 5 'huzzahs' that were to say 'long live the King'. The winds continued favorable for us. We aimed E 1/4 SE at full sail, the winds to west great and fresh, the sea a little rough, the view to starboard sometimes quite beautiful.

The 10th of November – At 2 o'clock in the afternoon the winds WNW big and fresh, cool and cloudy weather. The big sea making the ESE and E 1/4 SE under the two topsails and the foresail, having observed at midday the latitude of 49° 8 minutes, we knew of a leeward ship to us lying to under her main sail and the mizzen. We laid by to talk to him. At 3 o'clock he told us that *Belle Isle* at ENE at 25 leagues away.[120] We continued our route under the same sails until ten o'clock in the evening, when we sounded and found 66 fathoms of water and a bottom of fine gray sand with some alien tip. For this reason the topsails were taken in and we settled to the cape under main sail until midnight, then we hoisted the foresail, taking in the main sail, and sailed to the SE to find *Isle Dieu*, the winds at NW large and fresh by Grenans.[121] At 4 o'clock in the morning we set the two topsails and the main sail, the winds variable in the NNW, holding the route at SE 1/4 E and ESE, at 7 in the morning a clear day and sunny. We saw a ship in front of us on our route. We showed the truce flag for him, to speak to him, but he did not wait for us, seemingly taking us for an ill-intentioned ship.

The 13th at midday, having reached 46° 42 m[inutes], we made our route at ESE and E 1/4 SE full sails, clear weather, stormy seas and the winds to the NNW, variable to north and very fresh. At 2 o'clock we adjusted to ESE. At four o'clock we saw land before us four leagues distant, which we recognized as *Isle Dieu*.

Unsigned.

120 *Belle Isle*: Belle-Île-en-Mer, off the coast of Brittany.
121 *Isle Dieu*: Isle d'Yeu, west of the Loire region of France.

2

Jean-Claude Panet

Jean-Claude Panet is believed to have been born in Paris during late December of 1719. He sailed to New France in 1740, leaving La Rochelle on 10 June and landing at Québec on 12 August. He was 21 years old, apparently well-educated, and a soldier of the Colony troops. Within eight months of arriving he was already established as a legal practitioner and later as an attorney. Panet bought his release from the military in 1743 and was appointed royal notary in the provost court of Québec on 22 December 1744. In this position he would create official records of marriages, contracts and other legal documentation. He worked continuously as a notary from 1745 until 1775.

During the 1759 siege of Québec Panet had been named head of a commission charged with suppressing looting by sailors, soldiers and militia, and acted as a liaison between town and military officials. Later Panet would be one of 25 leading citizens to sign a request for capitulation addressed to the King's Lieutenant and *commandant* in Québec, Jean-Baptiste-Nicolas-Roch de Ramezay.

Following the surrender of Québec, Panet continued his work as a notary and was named chief clerk of a new court of final appeal for the District of Québec by the British governor, Major General James Murray. In 1767 he stepped down from this office and returned to work as a notary and lawyer, until 1775 when he was appointed as a 'keeper of the peace' and commissioner for the district of Québec, an appointment equivalent to a judgeship. In August 1776 Panet became a justice of the peace, and on 6 March 1777 a judge of the Court of Common Pleas. Jean-Claude Panet died on 28 February 1778, at 58 years of age.[1]

1 Jean-Claude Panet: André Frenière, 'Panet, Jean-Claude,' in *Dictionary of Canadian Biography*, vol.4 (Toronto: University of Toronto/Université Laval, 2003–).

The Siege of Québec in 1759[2]

10 May, 1759 – At seven o'clock in the evening a rumor spread through *Québec* that *M. de Bougainville* had arrived: it was true.[3] He actually landed at *M. de Bienne*'s, storekeeper, and went to find the *Intendant* [Bigot] at *M. Péan*'s, had a conference with him and did not deliver any news, otherwise we would hear of big events. *M. de Bougainville* re-embarked in the frigate *La Chézine*, Captain *Duclos*,[4] detached from Mr Kanon's fleet, two hundred leagues from France.

14 May – The frigate anchored in the harbor.

15 – *Sieur Dinel* arrived, second in command to *M. Kanon*, commander of the *frégate Le Marchault*,[5] whom I led to the *munitionnaire*.[6] He announced the happy news of the arrival of *M. Kanon*'s fleet, some at the *Isle aux Coudres*,[7] others at the post at *l'Eau de Vie*,[8] except for three they were worried about and had seen in the Gulf, which were: the *Duc de Fronsac*, the *Rameau* and *Nouvelle Rochelle*.[9] You cannot doubt the joy that this news gave us.

20 – This fleet arrived safely, with the exception of the three above. These ships, numbering three frigates and fifteen merchants (ships) did not bring us the nine to ten thousand quarters of flour, or so much bacon, but a lot of drinks and dry goods for the *munitionnaire*; the majority of the private goods were those of Messrs *Monnier*, *Lez*, and *Martin*, of wines and *eau de vie*.[10]

28 – The *Duc de Fronsac*, which had been feared lost, arrived richly loaded.

2 This translation has been completed using the French edition included in J.M. LeMoine (ed.), *Manuscripts Relating to the Early History of Canada*, 4th Series (Québec: Dawson & Co., 1875).

3 Bougainville: see footnote 20, p.19.

4 Duclos: see footnote 47, p.26.

5 The *Marchault* (Machault): see footnote 23, p.20 (Panet uses 'Machaux').

6 The *munitionnaire* was the purveyor general for the army, sourcing and supplying all food and supplies. Joseph-Michel Cadet held this position in New France at the time of the siege.

7 *Isle aux Coudres*: see footnote 32, p.21.

8 *L'Isle du Pot à l'Eau de Vie*: an island in the Rivière St Laurent estuary, near the current Saint-Siméon and l'Anse-au-Persil.

9 *Le Duc de Fronsac, Capitaine* Jaçques Villeur. 450 tons out of Bordeaux. Wrecked 23 November 1759. *Le Rameau, Capitaine* Louis Nadeau. 120–130 tons from Québec via Bordeaux. *La Nouvelle Rochelle*, unidentified, not appearing on related lists. Possibly *l'Amitié*, which hailed from Rochelle, *Capitaine* Michel François Voyer. 250–280 tons. Campeau, *Navires Venus en Nouvelle-France.*

10 *Eau de vie* is a light-flavored, colorless fruit brandy.

29 – Dufils Charest, commander frigate *Soleil Royal*, arrived from *Bayonne*, loaded with flour, peas, rice and *eau de vie.*[11]

June First – There have arrived the *Atalante*,[12] a frigate armed in Rochefort, with the flute *Marie*,[13] and the frigate *Pomone*, of Brest, with the *Pie*;[14] all loaded with munitions of war. From all the news and the statements of the prisoners taken on the *Pays d'en Haut*,[15] we were certain that we would be attacked, and that a siege of *Québec* was decided.

6 – I spoke to the captain of the flute *Marie*, who confirmed our idea, having reported that, passing north of *St Barnabé* (*Isle St Barnabé*), he had seen seven big ships anchored, to the south, and as the wind was good, we hoped in vain that it was the fleet coming from the islands.[16, 17] Before long we realized that it was the first division of the English, in front to intercept the relief bound for *Québec.*

7 – We heard from *M. Aubert* that there were seven English ships anchored at *St Barnabé.*[18]

8 – *M. de Léry*, detached to *Camouraskas*, tells us that the savages had assured him that there were more than sixty sails.[19] At the end of May *M. de Montcalm* arrived at *Québec*; his arrival heralded the certainty of a siege. *M. Général* (it is undoubtedly *Général de Lévis*) did not delay in coming. From the end of May until the end of June we did considerable work in *Québec*. We have added to all the batteries, we have established one at the Palace; we made considerable entrenchments at *Beauport*, from *Montmorency* to the passage of the *Petite Rivière*, on which has been established a pontoon bridge, and where five battalions of regular troops are encamped, with (those of) the Colony and Militia. All ships, except frigates and King's flutes, were disarmed and destined to be burned. *M. Kanon*'s fleet will sail

11 Joseph Charest (Charet) dit Dufils: see footnote 61, p.29.

12 The *Atalante*: see footnote 60, p.29.

13 The *Marie, Capitaine* Cornillaud (Cornille), armed *en flûte*, meaning the armament has been reduced and the ship designated as a transport vessel. 'List of ships of the line of France,' *Wikipedia.*

14 *La Pie, Capitaine* Duvilliers, 320 tons out of Rochefort, armed *en flûte*. Left Bordeaux 22 March 1759 and arrived at Québec 22 May 1759. Richard Couture, 'Pie (18),' *Kronoskaf Seven Years War Project*, http://www.kronoskaf.com/syw/index.php?title=Pie_(18) (accessed 7 December 2018).

15 *Pays d'en Haut*: literally the 'upper country,' refers to the wilderness areas frequented only by the fur traders.

16 Isle St Barnabé in the Rivière St Laurent NE of Québec City, at present-day Rimouski.

17 Inserts with parentheses throughout are editorial additions in the 1875 publication.

18 Ignace-Philippe Aubert de Gaspé: see footnote 30, p.21.

19 Gaspard-Joseph Chaussegros de Léry: see footnote 36, p.21.

and be taken to safe harbor at *St Anne de Batiscan*;[20] as well as the *St Augustin de Bilboa*,[21] the *Atalante*, by *M. Vogorties*; the flute *La Pie*, by *M. Sauran*,[22] and the *Duc de Fronsac*, will be near the *Richelieu*.[23] We built two boats, armed with four 24-pound guns, called 'troublemakers,' seven boats mounted with 24-pound guns, and a floating battery of *M. Guyot*'s invention, mounted with twelve pieces of cannon, four of 24, four of 18, and four of 12 pounds.[24] All these works, as well as the fireships and a large number of fire rafts, will be ready before the enemy is in front of the city. We learned that the English had made their descent to *Isle aux Coudres*, and settled there.

9 – A detachment has been formed of about 60 Abenaki savages and 60 Canadians, commanded by *M. de Niverville*;[25] *Sieur Desrivières*,[26] who had come from France, was with him as a volunteer. The savages amuse themselves on the *Isle d'Orléans* eating the beef and sheep abandoned there. *Isle d'Orléans* was abandoned in a hurry, a rush that does not bring honor to those in charge there. It was the same from the south coast to the *Rivière-du-Loup*, to *Pointe de Lévy*. *M. Desrivières*, who did not want to return without having done anything, broke off with seven Canadians from *Isle aux Coudres* who had taken refuge at *St Joachim*, and settled on the *Isle*, where he waited in ambush.

10 – They [M. Desrivières and his men] took three young people, including the grandson of the commander of the fleet of seven large vessels, a marine guard and another officer riding on horseback past their ambush to place the English flag on a height, who had their horses killed from under them and were made prisoners.

12 – These three young people were brought to *Québec*, where the commander's grandson was separated, he was found to speak French well. They were interrogated and by their statements confirmed the siege of *Québec*; that they must have twenty-five ships of the line, twelve frigates and two hundred transport ships; that they estimate twenty thousand men are coming; that they felt certain of taking *Québec*, thinking that all our regulars (regular troops) were at Carillon, where they would be beaten by three thousand men who would then join the fleet; and they count this operation as well as done. These young men were treated honorably

20 Ste Anne de Batiscan: on the Batiscan River of the northern shore of the Rivière St Laurent SW of Québec City.

21 *St Augustin de Bilboa*: 400 tons out of Bordeaux. Campeau, *Navires Venus en Nouvelle-France*.

22 Mssrs Vogorties and Sauran could not be identified.

23 The Richelieu River intersects the Rivière St Laurent well south of Québec City, at Sorel.

24 Panet lists a M. Gayot as the designer of the floating battery, surely intending Pierre-Nicolas Guyot, *dit* Duclos, captain of La Chézine, and has been corrected.

25 Joseph-Claude Boucher de Niverville: see footnote 41, p.23.

26 Eustache Trottier Desrivières: see footnote 42, p.23.

for seven to eight days in *Québec*, and then we transferred them to *Trois-Rivières*. They rented from the Canadians who had killed their horses without incident.

14 – We learned that they (the English) had tried to land two barges at *Baie St Paul*, but were driven off by the inhabitants.

From the 14th until the 20th of June many preparations were made to receive the enemy, our having learned that more than sixty ships had crossed.

21 – Three frigates appeared within sight of *Québec* and sailed into the bay at *l'Anse du Fort* and at *Trou* (*Trou de St Patrice, Isle d'Orléans*).[27, 28]

24 – Strong north-east [winds]; they lost a big vessel on the flats near *l'Anse du Fort*, but they saved the cargo. Seven other small transport vessels floundered in the *Trou*, most of which were lost. The English officers were seen to anchor their large ships where we have customarily anchored our merchant ships, their having anchored south of *Pointe de Lévy*, opposite the church at the beach in *Beaumont*.

> Announcement by His Excellency James Wolfe, Major General of Infantry, Commander-in-Chief of the Troops of His Britannic Majesty on the Rivière St Laurent: the King, my master, justifiably irritated with France, has resolved to set aside pride, and to avenge the insults to the English Colonies; he is also determined to send a formidable sea and land force that locals will see advance to the center of their country. Its purpose is to deprive the Crown of France the most considerable establishments which it enjoys in North America. It is to this end that he has sent me to this country at the head of the formidable army currently under my command. Farmers, settlers and peasants, women, children, the sacred religious ministers are not the object of the resentment of the King of Great Britain; it is not against them he raises his arm; he foresees their calamities, understands their fate, and offers them a helping hand.
>
> Inhabitants are allowed to come to their families, in their homes. I promise them my protection and assure they can, without fearing the least molestations, enjoy their property, follow the worship of their religions; in other words, in the middle of the war enjoy all the benefits of peace: provided they undertake no direct or indirect share in a dispute that effects only the two crowns. If, on the contrary, a stubbornness

27 *L'Anse du Fort*: a natural cove at the southernmost tip of Isle d'Orléans.

28 *Trou de St Patrice*: a cove and river estuary on the SE coast of Isle d'Orléans, at present-day Village-des-Anglais. Trou St Patrice is a colloquialism for St Patrick's Hole, an Irish cave by which he is said to have passed into hell.

and a recklessness makes them take up arms, they can expect to suffer all the cruelties that war offers. It is easy for them to imagine the fury of an unrestrained soldier; our orders alone can stop the course, and it is for Canadians, by their conduct, to obtain this advantage. They can not ignore their present situation; a formidable fleet blocks the passage of any assistance they could hope for from Europe, and a large army presses them from landward. The path they must take is certain; what can they expect from a vain and blind opposition? They must judge for themselves. The unheard-of cruelties which the French have exercised against Britain's subjects established in America could serve as an excuse for the most severe retribution; but the Englishman reproves a barbarous method. Their religion only preaches humanity, and his heart gladly follows the precept.

If the mad hope to successfully repel us leads the Canadians to refuse the neutrality that I propose to them, and gives them the presumption of appearing arms in hand, they will only have themselves to blame when they will groan under the weight of the misery to which they will suffer by their own choice. It will be too late to regret their unnecessary military efforts when, during the winter, they will see famine, etc., [afflict] all that they hold dear. As for me, I will not have anything for which to reproach myself. The rights of war are known, and the stubbornness of an enemy provides the means by which one applies reason.

It is permissible for the people of Canada to choose; on one side, England is giving them a powerful and helpful hand; its faithfulness in fulfilling its commitments, and she offers to ensure the inhabitants their rights and their possessions. On the other side, France, incapable of supporting this people, abandons their cause in the most critical moment, and if during the war she sent them troops, what were they used for? To make them feel with more bitterness the weight of a hand that oppresses instead of rescues them. Canadians should choose wisely; their fate depends on their choice.

Given at our Headquarters, *St Laurent* Parish, *Isle d'Orléans*, 27 June 1759.

From the 27th to the 29th, different preparations were made to send seven fire-ships, including three big merchant vessels, other *goélettes* and *bâteaux*.[29, 30] Commanding the fireships, the *Sieur Delouche*, commander of the merchant ship *l'Américain*.[31] The same day, it was decided by a council that *Sieur Delouche* would

29 *Goélettes*: schooners.

30 *Bâteaux*: boats: see footnote 52, p.26.

31 *François Delouche (de Louches) de St-Denis*: see footnote 55, p.28. Text uses 'Sieur Oclouches', likely a typographical error.

burn or chase the three frigates that were the advance guard, and that the others, after they had weighed anchor, would set fire to the fleet of sixty ships that was anchored in three lines above the *Trou* (*le Trou de St Patrice.*)

The plan was good, but poorly executed. *Sieur Delouche* set his fire after passing *Pointe de Lévy* to the south, and the three frigates were anchored to the north; they continued to sail, however, and the fireship grounded at *Beaumont*. Of the six others there were only four who fired between the two points, of which the best, *Sieur Dubois*,[32] who set his fire first and jumped, the other two fired at the sight of *Québec*, so that the English who in the beginning were dismayed, shouted 'Hurray!' and mocked our operations.

30 – The enemy appeared in sight of *Québec* and anchored two frigates and a *bâteau* in the basin (the harbor), out of cannon range. It is notable that since the arrival of the English fleet, each was at his station, and the Reserve company was not forgotten.

1st of July – The English sent out an officer in a launch from the frigate, which stopped in the middle of the basin, by two boats that were in front of him. He handed them a letter by which they gave notice that they had taken several Acadian ladies in Miramichi,[33] including *Madame Pomeray*, *Mme St Villemin* among them, as well as *Mme Beaumont*, her daughter and daughter-in-law, whom they had sent back, and that they were ready to dismiss the others, and inquired of the three prisoners from *Isle aux Coudres*. On the same day the *Chevalier Le Mercier*, charged with the reply, which he carried aboard the first frigate that stood in front of him. It stated that the General had no doubt about the courtesy of the Admiral toward the ladies; he thanked him; that he had treated the prisoners with distinction, and that as soon as the Admiral is kind enough to inform him of his departure, that he would send them back to him.

It is to be observed that the English had seized *Isle d'Orléans*, where they seemed to have made their general disembarkation, and camped there. The same day we learned that *M. de Léry*, who had been detached to evacuate the inhabitants of the south coast, had been surprised with its inhabitants by the English who had landed at *Beaumont*; despite their surprise, they threw themselves upon their weapons, killed two Englishmen and saved themselves. We only lost two men, we do not know if they are killed or taken prisoner. *M. de Léry* has lost his sword and several papers he had spread over a table.

From the 20th of June until the 1st of July, we went down to about 300 Outaouais and 400 Iroquois and Abenaki. On the news of the English landing at *Beaumont*,

32 *Honoré Dubois de la Militère*: see footnote 57, p.28.

33 The Mirimichi River area in New Brunswick, an Acadian refugee area following their expulsion after the June 1755 French losses of Forts Beauséjour and Gaspereau.

M. Charest, a zealous patriot, asked *M. le Gouverneur-Général* to meet the English, and prevent their establishment at *Pointe de Lévy.*[34] He was told that he could go if he thought it appropriate. He went with about twenty inhabitants of *Pointe de Lévy*; he was very surprised arriving at his house to see English on the main road, whom he took at first for inhabitants. He was not disconcerted; although he saw about four hundred men, he rallied with about forty men, fired on them and killed ten without losing a single man. He retreated into the woods, sent for balls and powder; it was quickly sent to him; he began a small engagement and was obliged to withdraw on the same day. The English who appeared with full strength on *Isle d'Orléans* had not yet landed three thousand men at *Pointe de Lévy. M. Charest* requested a thousand to twelve hundred men to prevent their establishment. His repeated requests were for nil.

3 – He was there with about thirty inhabitants of *Pointe de Lévy* and *Sieur LeGris*, volunteer, and thirty Abenaki savages.[35] They struck; killed about thirty. The Savages took eight scalps and brought back a prisoner. The savages, by (lack of) caution, lost four men by returning to the King's Road, where there were more than [blank space] soldiers. On the same day, it was decided in the Council that fifteen hundred men would leave at night for *Pointe de Lévy*, but this unfortunate prisoner's statement deranged the plan, for which we feared unfortunate consequences. The prisoner testified that they had about a thousand regular troops there and that the same night they plan to attack *Beauport.* All the camp as well as the city turned out, consequently, and camped on the lines all night; nothing bad happened.

4 – We noticed a great movement in the fleet during the night, and there was a large transport from *Pointe de Lévy* to *Isle d'Orléans.* In consequence *Sieur Charest* proposed to go on reconnaissance; it was actually the night of the 4th to the 5th, with the *Sieur LeGris* and twelve inhabitants; he returned on the 5th and reported that the camp at *Pointe de Lévy*, established between the mill and the church, was almost empty; that there were only a few advanced positions and that there could be no more than 800 men. He asked the *Gouverneur-Général*, uselessly, to be able to take volunteers. He did not wish to let him. For evidence of his mission he took, with *Sieur LeGris*, four haversacks brought back from the enemy camp.

5 – It was noticed in the city that the enemy constructed camps of considerable size, despite the few people they had, and were not deterred. The Ottawa savages

34 This is an assumption as to the person intended. As in the Foligné manuscript, *le Général* appears to refer to Vaudreuil. Here Panet has written '*M. le Général de monde*'. I am interpreting it as indicating the top general.

35 *Pierre-Denis LeGris*: see footnote 62, p.29.

returned, having grown considerably in strength to the number of 100, but without success, and having killed only a few Englishmen.

6th and 7th – The works continued and we saw clearly that they were building a battery at the *Citière*,[36] opposite the castle, twelve pieces of cannon and 7 mortars from 10 to 13 inches, and a retrenchment above, with ditches and palisades to hold 200 men. The 7th, at night, *Sieur Charest* was again out scouting. On the 8th he reported that he had seen the beginning of these works closely; that there could be about 300 workers and 500 armed men to support them.

An Englishman previously taken at Chouaguin,[37] who had served an English officer at *Chalou*, profited by a canoe being left at the edge of the water, and there being a sentinel, told his comrade that he was going to fetch fish from the fisheries, and as they realized that he wanted to desert, two *barques* got in front and intercepted him. He testified that there were only about 800 men at *Pointe de Lévy*; come to transport cannon, and that two Royal American regiments that had landed at *Pointe de Lévy* did not want to work or fight, saying they had not been paid for thirteen months, they had been told that they were only being transported to Canada to give them housing; that they had made a landing of 1,500 men at *St Joachim*, who had to come by way of the woods, who would join the bulk of the army, which was to remain at *Beauport*; that the English who were but 10,000, expected 6,000 reinforcements from Martinique.

We are active on the banks as far as the area of *l'Ange-Gardien*, with two batteries they anchored in the north channel.[38] They had four big vessels to support their attack, who fired without any success for four hours.

Several cannon shots and bombs landed on the works at *Pointe de Lévy*, but I think, rather uselessly.

On the same day it was discovered that the British were trying a landing by the *Sault de Montmorency*, at low tide.[39] The Outaouais savages happily went there, to the number of 200, with some Canadians. They met a detachment of 100 Englishmen who were almost destroyed; they (the English) fell back on 300 men, were fired upon by the savages, where they (the English) lost this world. This second party having dropped back, the savages pursued them with tomahawks, but being too engaged in taking scalps, they received about 4,000 gunshots. They lost only three men; five wounded; one of their interpreters named *Hause Le Fleau* was killed, and two Canadians. Immediately a detachment from *M. de Lévy*'s camp was set to guard the passage of the *Sault* from above. The same day the city

36 I find no clear reference to La Citière on period maps.

37 Oswego.

38 *L'Ange Gardien*: see footnote 97, p.48.

39 *Sault de Montmorency*: see footnote 29, p.20.

received a mortar from *de Lévy*'s camp, which fired at eight o'clock in the evening and obliged the English ships to withdraw with the first two.

That same day twenty-three deserters from *St Antoine* came to us, who, after their having been well-received, told stories that made us laugh.[40] One says that Louisbourg was retaken by the French, and that the English fleet was in disarray and gathering to leave; another that the King of Prussia lost 20,000 men in a battle, and that the Queen of Hungary was mistress of Silesia and the French of the Hanover Electorate. Finally, that Admiral Saunders had given General Wolfe until the end of the month to make his final efforts. I think it's on this statement that we could count the most.

The 10th saw our batteries aimed on the camp at *Pointe de Lévy*; it did not appear that this prevented their operations, although fire continued at night. The same day, there was a small skirmish at the *Sault*, where there were about twenty English killed; we only lost one savage.

The same day, an English deserter arrived at camp at 9 o'clock in the evening, having passed from *Isle d'Orléans* to *l'Ange Gardien*, and passed through the woods where he found the priest who brought him in. We learn nothing from him.

The 11th, the English batteries were noted as being complete. The *chèvres* were there to mount the guns.[41] At noon we saw them draw in their cannons.

A detachment of 500 Canadians, 100 men of Colony troops, and 60 volunteers of various regiments, commanded by *M. Dumas*,[42] was sent from the camp below *Beauport* to *Pointe de Lévy*, to seize the English battery; this party did not leave the same day; we informed the General.

12 – The party was increased by about 350 men from the city, volunteers, of which 17 were men of the reserve company, commanded by *M. Glemet*.[43] *M. Duchesnay*[44] made excuses for going.

40 *St Antoine*: see footnote 103, p.50.

41 *Chèvre* or *chevrette*, literally a goat, is an old French slang for a machine used to lift guns onto their carriages.

42 *Jean-Daniel Dumas*: see footnote 75, p.35.

43 Likely intending Pierre Glemet, a Huguenot merchant at Québec specializing around this time in seal hunting for oil and skins. Information gleaned from several entries in the online *Dictionary of Canadian Biography*, including: François Rousseau, 'Vienne, François-Joseph de,' in *Dictionary of Canadian Biography*, vol.4 (Toronto: University of Toronto/Université Laval, 2003–).

44 I believe this to be Antoine Juchereau Duchesnay (1740–1806). Army and militia officer, *seigneur* and politician. Listed in 1760 as an *enseigne* in the colonial regular troops, given a special assignment by Bougainville. He would go on to become a wealthy man, much of which he lost during Benedict Arnold's 1775 invasion. Réal Brisson, 'Juchereau Duchesnay, Antoine,' in *Dictionary of Canadian Biography*, vol.5 (Toronto: University of Toronto/Université Laval, 2003–).

This detachment went to *Sillery* in the daytime, and at nine o'clock at night they successfully crossed. Hardly had the advanced guard marched when some schoolchildren (students of the *séminaire de Québec*), startled, fired at the top of a deep ravine onto their friends. It is said that, from this false alarm, about 600 deserted. Having climbed and gained a second footing, some soldiers from *Roussillon* (from the 'Royal Roussillon' regiment) raised a new alarm, shouting to those who were in line that the English cavalry was marching, which again caused men to retreat. Finally, for the most part, it was only *M. Dumas*, with the reserve company and about 300 men, who approached within a rifle's shot and a half of the British entrenchments.

That same night, at nine o'clock in the evening, the English began to fire on *Québec* and bomb the city; every half an hour they fired five cannon shots and as many bombs. A *galliote* in front of *Pointe de Lévy* threw in a few.[45] She stood together with several other ships on the same line.

13 – The English continued the bombardment.

14 – The detachment commanded by *M. Dumas* ran into *M. Lefebvre*'s servant, he was killed there by our people.[46]

The 15th, the bombardment continued at *Québec*; the parish and the Jesuits were the most damaged; *Sieur Amiot*'s house, in the lower town, was riddled with cannon shots; the church of the lower town took several balls.[47]

16 – The English threw a fire-pot on the *Chevalier*'s house; the fire took hold of it, communicated to that of *M. Moran*, beyond to that of *Chennevert*, that of *Girard*, behind to that of *Cardoneau*, *Dacier*, of *Madame de Boishébert*. All these houses were consumed by fire. That of *Cardoneau*, the remaining ceiling of the ground floor stood firm. The vaults have not been damaged; they are fortunate. May God preserve them from accident!

17 – *Collet*, a merchant and officer in *M. Parent*'s battery, who was in front of his house, was killed by a cannonball, as well as *Gauvreau*, the cooper. A man named

45 *Galliotes à bombes*: see footnote 49, p.26.

46 While the servant cannot be identified, this is most likely a reference to a noted Québec merchant and trader, a Huguenot named Jean LeFebvre. Dale Miquelon, 'Lefebvre, Jean', in *Dictionary of Canadian Biography*, vol.3 (Toronto: University of Toronto/Université Laval, 2003–).

47 Jean-Baptiste Amiot (1717–1769): wealthy Québec merchant, supplier to the state. Elected in 1759 as churchwarden in the parish council of Notre-Dame de Québec. After the conquest he was one of the people overseeing the re-establishment of the religious institutions in the colony. José Igartua, 'Amiot, Jean-Baptiste (1717–69)', in *Dictionary of Canadian Biography*, vol.3 (Toronto: University of Toronto/Université Laval, 2003–).

Pouliot, of *St Foi*, was crushed by a bomb that obliterated him. Two men were wounded, *Brassard* and *Dufour*.

The English have built a battery of 50 guns at the *Sault*.

The same day, in the night, there were killed by the Outaouais savages, in different actions, about 60 men in *Sault Montmorency*. They took three prisoners who report that at *Pointe de Lévy* there were not more than 700 men; that they were about 7,000 at *l'Ange Gardien*; that they were worried about thirty ships said to be on the river.

18 – At midnight there was an alarm. A two-decked ship, three frigates and two *bâteaux* passed in front of the city aided by the dark night. One frigate ran aground on *Pointe de Lévy*. It is thought that she cannot be freed. These vessels were anchored at *l'Anse des Mères*.[48] They have detached a frigate to scout a fire-ship, the only one remaining. Having recognized it, and finding no one there, they have detached a barge to set it on fire. They keep our rafts which have been ready for fifteen days and are not yet loaded.

The same night *M. Villegoint*,[49] officer, arrived at *Québec*, coming from *Miramichi* with *M. Boishébert*[50] and about 300 men, both Canadian, Acadian, and low-country savages.

In the morning, *M. Dumas* was sent out with about 600 men to observe their movements, and 100 men have carried some field guns. We also sent a letter to warn our frigates and vessels anchored at *Platon*,[51] and four across from the *Batiscan*.[52]

20 – The English have detached barges carrying about 1,200 grenadiers, Scots, and Highlanders, who were descending toward the mill and the church at *Pointe aux Trembles* in the night, without being spotted.[53] On the same day the English continued to fire their cannon and bomb the city.

48 *L'Anse des Mères*: see footnote 85, p.39.

49 Possibly Commander of Port La Joye, Raymond de Villejoint, from Isle St Jean, now Prince Edward Island, at the time of the 1758 French surrender of Isles Royale and St Jean. Rameau de Saint-Père, *Une Colonie Féodale en Amérique L'Acadie (1604–1881)*, vol.2 (Montréal: Granger Frères, 1889), p.225; and Lucie LeBlanc Consentino, 'Hundreds perish at sea while being deported', Acadian & French-Canadian Ancestral Home, http://www.acadian-home.org/acadians-die-at-sea.html (accessed 1 January 2019).

50 Charles Deschamps de Boishébert et de Raffetot (1727–1797): officer of Colonial regular troops with a long history of service in Acadia. Phyllis E. Leblanc, 'Deschamps de Boishébert et de Raffetot, Charles', in *Dictionary of Canadian Biography*, vol.4 (Toronto: University of Toronto/Université Laval, 2003–).

51 *Pointe Platon*: on the Rivière St Laurent's south shore between Ste Croix and Lotbinière, extending 6 km into the Rivière St Laurent, deflecting river currents and prevailing winds for a secure anchorage.

52 *Batiscan* on the Rivière St Laurent's north shore, located at the junction of the Rivière St Laurent and Batiscan River, north of Trois Rivières and across the river from present-day St Pierre les Becquets.

53 *Pointe aux Trembles*:see footnote 86, p.40.

21 – At half-past three in the morning the twelve hundred men have landed at *Pointe aux Trembles*. They were fired on by about 40 savages, where they lost six or seven men and as many wounded. They surrounded the houses near the church and they made three men prisoners, including *Sieur La Casse*, sleeping with *Madame Landry*, who had left the reserve company under pretense of sore legs, was of the number. He was caught on the street in a gown (judge of his good morals) with *Sieur Laîné* and *Sieur Frichet*. They took about thirteen women of the city refugees at the said place, being the Ladies *Duchesnay*, *De Charnay*, his mother, his sister. *Mlle Couillard*, the Joly, Mailhot, and Magnan families were among them. They treated them with all possible politeness. General Wolfe was at the head, and Mr Stobo[54] was there, who paid many compliments.

The sad thing is that the English had done them no wrong, and that the savages pillaged the houses and almost all the property of these refugee families. Poor *Michaud* was shot in the cheek. The English left most of the other women, and especially pregnant ones.

22 – About nine o'clock they sent a representative to *l'Anse des Mères* to offer to return all women, provided we let pass a small boat loaded with their sick and wounded. This offer was accepted. We were receiving women at *l'Anse des Mères* at three o'clock in the morning, and who were welcomed with great politeness. Each officer gave his name to the beautiful prisoners as they met. The English had promised not to bombard or bomb until nine o'clock in the evening, to give the women the time to retreat to where they would judge appropriate, but that past this hour, they would fire at will. They kept their word; at nine o'clock they fired for a quarter hour, ten or twelve bombs, which were returned with skill. They set fire to the Parish (the parish church) and to *M. Rotot*'s house. The Parish as well as the houses from M. *Duplessis* to *M. Imbert* (*rue La Fabrique*), and all the

54 Robert Stobo (1726–1770), Scottish-born captain and regimental engineer with Washington at Fort Necessity in 1754, where he was one of two hostages turned over to the French. During his time among the French Stobo accumulated information on Fort Duquesne and Québec City, having free movement within them. In 1757 Stobo escaped twice, and was recaptured twice. On 1 May 1759, he finally succeeded, escaping by canoe with eight other American prisoners, and 36 days later sailing the group into British-held Louisbourg on a captured schooner, with two French captains held prisoner. Quickly assigned to General Wolfe's staff, Stobo would act as guide during the 21 July attack on Pointe aux Trembles. In his memoir, Stobo claims to have shown General Wolfe the approach to the Plains of Abraham used in the 13 September landing. Stobo would miss the fall of Quebec, having been sent first with messages to General Amherst at Crown Point, and then continuing south to his home in Williamsburg, Virginia. Stobo later became an officer in the British army and led his company into Montréal on 11 September 1760. Stobo continued to serve in Canada, Cuba and was finally stationed in Chatham, England, where on 19 June 1770, he took his own life following a series of personal setbacks and chronic alcoholism. Robert C. Alberts, 'Stobo, Robert', in *Dictionary of Canadian Biography*, vol.3 (Toronto: University of Toronto/Université Laval, 2003–), http://www.biographi.ca/en/bio/stobo_robert_3E.html (accessed 20 June 2019).

back houses, including my own (*rue St Joseph*) which occupied *Francheville*, are included, having been consumed by the flames. Fortunately, almost no one has been killed, with the exception of a gunner who, having put the *gargousse* in a too hot gun, was killed.[55] A bomb fell on Mr *Ouillame*'s house, which injured the maid at the thigh and mortally wounded a man.

23 – At four o'clock in the morning the English tried to pass two frigates in front of the city; but our gunfire forced them to retire. They barely fired their guns all day.

24 – The British started bombarding and firing on the city.

25 – On the considerable thefts which have happen at *Québec*, by the sailors, soldiers and militia, I suggested to *M. Daine* that it was necessary for the Governor and the Intendant to pass an order that looters be summarily hanged.[56] The plan which had been drawn up of the ordinance and which was along these terms was approved and followed. I was appointed clerk of the commission. The English continued to bombard and shell.

> His Excellency, stung by the little regard that the residents of Canada had of his advice on the 27th instant of last month, has resolved to no longer listen to the human sentiments which led him to relieve people blinded by their own misery. Canadians are showing their conduct to be unworthy of the advantages they have been given. That is why he ordered the commander of his light troops and other officers to go out into the country, to seize and bring in the inhabitants and their herds, and destroy and overthrow as they judge appropriate. As for the rest, being loath to adopt barbaric extremes which Canadians and their Indians allies have shown him by example, he proposes to postpone until August first next the decision on the fate of the prisoners that can be done, with which he will retaliate; unless during this interval Canadians do not submit to the terms he proposed to them in his advice, and by their submission,

55 *Gargousse*: a cartridge, the powder charge for a piece of artillery, usually contained in a paper or fabric outer covering.

56 François Daine, the lieutenant general for civil and criminal affairs of the provost court of Québec. With Jean Taché he headed the bourgeoisie delegation pushing for a citizens expedition on 12 July 1759 against an English battery. As lieutenant of the provost court he received a special commission permitting him to execute thieves after summary trial, an idea alleged to have come from Panet. After the Battle on the Plains of Abraham Daine became the spokesman for the townspeople, asking for the surrender of the town, to avoid the horrors of an assault; on this occasion he called himself 'mayor' of the town. Jacques Mathieu, 'Daine, François', in *Dictionary of Canadian Biography*, vol.3 (Toronto: University of Toronto/ Université Laval, 2003–).

claim his clemency and benefit from it. At St Henry, 25 July 1759. Joseph Dailling, Major Light Troops.

(A proclamation by General Wolfe)

A party of Ottawa and savages of different nations passed *Sault Montmorency*, made themselves known to the enemy and hid. The English who had noticed their maneuver paraded in two columns, about 1,500 men to locate them. The savages waited patiently hidden for three hours and, having seen them in range, fired and killed about 60 men. *M. de Répentigny* asked *M. de Lévis* for 2,000 men, who, having to ask *M. le Général de Montcalm*, arrived too late. The consternation was so severe among the English that they fled shouting 'All is lost!'; but we did not take advantage of this blow. The English continued their bombardment all day and night. The damage was increasing day by day. The same day they opened a new battery of twelve guns above the *Cabane des Pères.*[57] We learned the same day that the English had sent a detachment to *St Henry* to look for provisions, where they took 200 women and the priest. They have returned *Mlle St Paul.*

28 July – Several cannon shots at the *Sault*, both on our part and those of the enemy. They have similarly continued the bombardment and shelling of the city.

29 – A man was hanged for theft. The bombardment and shelling continued.

30 – Continuation of the bombardment.

31 – Two soldiers whom I had arrested having taken a quarter of *eau de vie* from the cellar of *M. Soupiran* which they had rolled and put in *Charland*'s house, in the *St Roch* district, have been hanged at three o'clock in the afternoon.

At nine o'clock in the morning two frigates of about 30 guns each set out and were grounded at *Sault Montmorency*, on the eastern tip, and began to fire across our entrenchment. Another large 60-gun ship went into position behind them. At the same time they opened a battery of 30 guns. There is heavy fire from this battery and these three vessels. It is estimated that they fired more than 2,500 rounds from 6 a.m. until 5 p.m. From this continual fire we only had four men killed and about fifteen wounded. During this cannonade, to which we responded with the three pieces of cannon we had, which formed a small redoubt, we pierced the first frigate with more than 30 balls, flooded with water and keeling over,

57 *Cabane des Pères*: located on the shore of Pointe de Lévy directly across the river from *Pointe à Carcy*, the historic name given to a small stone cabin built at the base of the cliff in 1646 or 1647 by the Jesuit Fathers for shelter and eel fishing. The hut was the very first European habitation on the Rivière St Laurent's southern shore. David Gagné, 'Le secteur de la Traverse', *Ville de Lévis, Service du Patrimonie et Soutien à l'Urbanisme*, (Québec: January 2013), https://www.ville.levis.qc.ca/fileadmin/Documents_PDF/Histoire-secteur-Traverse.pdf (accessed 7 December 2018), p.2.

stranded. About 300 barges (English) left *Isle d'Orléans* and *Pointe de Lévy*, and put themselves into three lines between the two stranded vessels.

Anticipating a general attack, *M. de Montcalm* went to *Sault* to join *M. de Lévis*. Over the five hours 2,000 English disembarked, at low tide, from their barges, marched quickly and in good order toward our redoubt and battery, which had been abandoned half an hour previously for lack of rounds. They seized it, but wanting to advance to the entrenchments, they were held off by a Canadian fire of approximately 1,500 gunshots. These Canadians were supported by 1,500 regular troops. The rest of *Beauport* camp and the Canadians from the passages were in line, and we had about 12,000 men turn out; but what stands out, more [men] than there were [musket]balls at the camp. Fortunately these 2,000 [British]were so hotly received that they re-embarked in their barges with the same rush as they had come out. 5,000 English who walked with a solemn step, and in good order, and who passed the *Sault* ford in battle order, advanced only twice a musket's range, and withdrew, when they saw those barges re-embark. How lucky they [the English] did not know that there were no bullets at the camp! What negligence that there were none, and what misfortune there would have been, if the English had continued their attack. They fled into a cove, commanded by a height so that they could not go out anymore. In this engagement the English lost 200 men and as many injured. We buried 83. 260 muskets were brought to camp; many others were swept away at the rising tide. A Scottish captain was taken prisoner; he was hit by 4 bullets, including 3 in the body, without a doubt he is in a serious condition.[58] We lost about 10 men and about 20 injured.

The same day, we waited in *St Roch*, and heard a loud cry of women and children shouting 'Long live the King!' I climbed up, and I saw the first frigate completely on fire; shortly thereafter, a black smoke rose from the second, which then took fire. It's the English who fired it for fear that we would take advantage of it.

First of August – The savages and the Canadians, despite the defenses where they were told to go, fear being exposed to enemy cannon, from the first frigate burned and which the sea had extinguished, we salvaged bacon, flour, spades, pickaxes, bolts of *écarlatine* and many other things.[59] By this, one can judge that this vessel was rich.

The Scottish captain, held prisoner, said he was at the head of 50 grenadiers; that those who were with him were chosen men, but they had abandoned him; and there had been a great terror in the army. They continued to shell and bombard the city.

58 Captain David Ochterlony: see footnote 90, p.46.

59 *Écarlatine*: a high-quality woolen fabric.

2 – They did the same until two o'clock in the afternoon, then they stopped, and from there until six in the evening, having sent an envoy on behalf of this Scottish officer who asked for his servant, his clothes and linen and money. We allowed him everything except his servant. At six o'clock, they continued their bombing with fury, to make up for lost time.

3 – We were afraid during the night, the movement of three large ships that were heading for the city, and by several who were filing along the *Lévy* coast, we feared another landing, either to the city or to *l'Anse des Mères*, but nothing new happened.

4 – Continuation of the bombing. They limited their shots to the upper and lower town; they sent some 80 rounds against the walls, and in the *St Roch* district.

5 – I left for *St Anne*, to see my wife. They had dispatched a courier for the three anchored vessels, which were the frigate commanded by *M. Vauquelain*,[60] the *Pie* by *M. Sauvage*,[61] and the *Duc de Fronsac* belonging to *M. Grani*.[62]

6 – These three vessels sailed and entered the Richelieu, and the English ships made no movement. These three vessels were anchored across from the church at Grondines. We learned that we had blown up the Forts *Carillon* and *St Frédéric* at the approach of 12,000 enemy men.[63] We only had 3,000. They reformed at *Isle aux Noix*.[64]

7 – The English attempted two landings at *Pointe aux Trembles*, one at 4 p.m., opposite the church, composed of about 200 men, who did not set foot on the ground and who lost about 60 men. *M. de Bougainville*, colonel and commander of grenadiers, realized that this attack was only a feint, having seen a large number of barges pass over. Indeed, he paraded his troops by following the barges, and seeing that the enemy wanted to land at the stream named the *Muletière*, half a league above the river *Jacques Cartier*, where we made entrenchments, he set his troops in ambush, in defensive positions, as they had not received orders. He could have 50 grenadiers, 300 regulars and 600 militiamen. The enemy at this landing might have had, by the estimate of their barges, about 1,200 men, who came with confidence to walk within twenty paces of our ambush, where they were received by a stunning fire; at the second discharge, the English barges returned to the open sea.

60 The *Atalante*, of the Royal Marine: see footnote 60, p.29.

61 The *Pie*, of the Royal Marine: 137. Perhaps a reassignment as *Capitaine* Sauvage arrived on the *Pomone*.

62 *Duc de Fronsac*, chartered to Cadet.

63 Southernmost French forts at Ticonderoga (Carillon) and Crown Point (St Frédéric).

64 *Isle aux Noix*: see footnote 95, p.48.

It is expected that they lost 200 men in this action, and as many wounded. *M. de Bougainville* assured me that he saw 7 barges in which he could see to have 50 men in each, and that he did notice in every barge 4 or 5 were rowing. The same day we learned of the capture of Niagara, and that the garrison was taken prisoner. It is feared that *M. de Caprenay* has suffered the same fate.

8 – After this action, the barges that had withdrawn, gained the south coast in the morning. 2 frigates were grounded to support their landing. 100 men that we had in this area fired three rounds to oppose their descent, but to no avail; they killed about 10 men, but they were forced to withdraw being cannonaded by ships and barges. The 1,200 men landed went down to *St Antoine*, to *Deruisseau*'s house.

The same day was fatal for me and for many others. The English, who had stopped cannonading and bombing since the 12th of July, when evening came they started again: they threw fire-pots on the lower town, three of which fell one on my house, one on a house at the Market Square, and one on Champlain Street. The fire took in three places. They fought the fires in vain, trying to put it out at my house, it spread a little north-east, and soon the lower town was nothing but a brazier; besides my house that of *M. Désery*, that of *Maillou*, *rue du Sault* to *Matelot*, all the lower town and all the *Cul-de-Sac* to the house of *Sr Voyer* who was spared, and finally to the house of *Sr DeVoisy*, everything was consumed by the flames.

There were 7 vaults that collapsed or burned, that of *M. Perrault*, the younger, that of *M. Tachet*,[65] of *M. Turpin*, of *Messrs Benjamin de La Mordic*, *Jehaune*, *Maranda*. Imagine the dismay. There were 167 houses burnt.

9 August – The English continued their bombardment, and have directed their bombs to the upper town.

10 – They did the same; and we sent a detachment of 500 men for the *Pays d'en Haut*.

11 – From our *Beauport* camp we formed a detachment of 300 Canadians and 300 savages to attack the workers who were above the *Sault*; instead of attacking these workers, they found 800 armed men who guarded them. Our party fought valiantly and killed about 150 men. The enemy retreated. We could have started a general action if we had supported our party and fell on the workers.

65 *Tachet*: most likely intending Jean-Pascal Taché, former militia captain, merchant and trader. A leader of the citizenry pressing for permission to attack a British battery on 12 July, and spokesperson for the merchants and townspeople requesting the commander surrender Québec without additional fighting following the 13 September battle. Mathieu, 'Daine, François'.

That night there was an alert: three frigates tried to pass with a small *galliote*. The three frigates retreated under fire of our guns and our mortar; the little schooner passed; she ran aground nevertheless, and 5 boats armed with 2 guns pursued her, but she got free and continued on her way.

12 – Despite a constant rain the English continued to shell and bombard. Since the 10th, they have sent 80 bombs, and their *carcasses*, which they have without doubt put in a large mortar, above the *Porte St Louis*,[66] in *St Valier* Street, and near the tents of the commissary, *M. Corpron*, acting as *munitionnaire* and the storekeeper camped in front of the *Hôpital Général*, below the Plains of Abraham. That same night, there was an alert: a soldier who reported shooting at *l'Anse des Mères*; he was mistaken. It was at the *Rivière des Etchemins*.

13 – The British directed their bombs at two vessels stranded on the *Rivière St Charles* as batteries, at the entrance to *Rivière St Charles*, making a continual fire, as well as their batteries from *Sault Montmorency*; despite that, there are only 40 men killed by cannon and bombs, both in the *Sault* and in the city, and so many maimed.

14 – Continuation of the fire from *Pointe de Lévy* on the city. Two sailors killed on the ramparts of *M. Nau*'s battery.

15 – The English have reduced their fire, and have fired almost no bombs.

16 – They fired little during the day, but in the evening they threw a lot of bombs and fire-pots of which one, about nine o'clock at night, set fire to the widow *Pinguet*'s house, across from the walls of the *Récollets*.[67] This fire was attended quite well as I saw it. Two *Recollect* brothers and two carpenters prevented the fire from spreading, by climbing on *Planty*'s neighboring house and discovering, despite the bombs and cannons, in what direction the fire was heading. There was no one wounded, and *M. Lusignan* and I were forced to leave for fear,[68] two bullets having grazed us, and a tile from the *Récollets*, detached by a cannonball from their roof above the church, having passed between Brother *Noël* and me.

66 *Porte St Louis*: on the Rue St Louis, facing west toward the Heights of Abraham.

67 *Récollets*: see footnote 87, p.42.

68 Possibly Paul-Louis Dazemard (Dassemat, Dazmard, Dazmat) de Lusignan (1691–1764) apparently also known as Louis-Antoine. 1705 cadet, 1712 *enseigne*, 1721 *lieutenant-en-second*, 1734 *lieutenant*, 1744 *capitaine*, 1757 *lieutenant* in the Royal Artillery. Long-time commander at Fort St Frédéric, 1749–1758. The two biographies differ on when he was returned to France following the surrender of Canada. J.R. Turnbull, 'Dazemard de Lusignan, Paul-Louis', in *Dictionary of Canadian Biography*, vol.3 (Toronto: University of Toronto/Université Laval, 2003–); and Government of Canada, 'Database of the 1759–1760 soldiers'.

17 – We found out this morning that four English boats detached themselves from the fleet and rejoined the vessels at the *Sault*; we did not doubt that it was to re-embark part of their artillery; indeed, they worked there all day and fired few guns from there. The English fire at *Pointe de Lévy* has begun; they fired up to 12 rounds every half an hour. What were they shooting at? On the sad debris of the fire of the lower town. There was this day a *pilotin* killed at *M. Glemet*'s house.[69]

18 – The English made a landing at *Deschambault*, at *M. Perrault*'s house, captain of that place.[70] This house served as a retirement home for the respected Amazon adventurer, *Madame Cadet*, wife of *Sieur Joseph Ruffio*.

This house was rich, several officers having stored their trunks there, which, as well as the house, could not be saved from the fire. During this operation, 15 cavalrymen, at the head of which was the *Sieur Beaucourt*, major of the cavalry, presented themselves boldly.[71] The English thought, no doubt, it was an advanced guard and embarked. This encouraged the little party that came to help, made up of about 300 men from *Cap Santé*.[72] The English were nearly 800; they lost 22 men, without including the wounded. We only had one Canadian injured, slightly. It should be noted that *M. de Montcalm* appeared after this noble expedition.

The English crossed with their barges to *Ste Croix*,[73] and they razed the countryside as they went. *M. Cournoyer*, officer of the colony, having 75 men with him, posted his troops in ambush, and ordered them to shoot at the first barge; which they did. They passed by them, and they killed about 200 without a return volley, since they did not see those who were shooting at them.

19 – The English again began to bombard the city, and to set fire to the areas of *St Antoine* and *Ste Croix*.

20 – It was found that the four English ships anchored at *Écureuils* have set out,[74] and were preparing to pass in front of the city, having covered their ships with large pieces of wood. Continuation of the gunfire at the city, and 2 sailors killed.

21 – The English, as is their custom, have set fire to *St Joachim*,[75] and burned both farms. Continuous cannonading of the city.

69 *Pilotin*: an apprentice river pilot in the merchant navy, training for a future post as a port officer.

70 *M. Perrault*: see footnote 109, p.53. Panet uses 'M. Perrot'.

71 See footnote 107, p.52 for cavalry information, see footnote 108, p,52 for Roche Beaucourt. Panet uses 'Sieur Belcour'.

72 *Cap Santé*: on the north shore of the Rivière St Laurent, just west of Jacques Cartier.

73 *Ste Croix*: on the south shore of the Rivière St Laurent, below Jacques Cartier.

74 *Écureuils*: on the northern shore of the Rivière St Laurent just east of Jacques Cartier.

75 *St Joachim*: see footnote 112, p.56.

22 – They set fire to the mill at the *Sault*, and the whole area of *Petit Pré* and *Château Richer*.[76]

23 The fire in these areas continued, we watched it all night. The same day I went for a walk in the lower town. We fired a dozen bombs on the English, and 20 cannon rounds, and they ceased their fire all the afternoon.

24 – *M. St Laurent* was sent at 7 o'clock in the morning, as an envoy for the dead Scottish officer, injured in the attack at the *Sault* on the 31st.[77] He made his will, by which he gave all his money and his effects to the soldier of *Languedoc* who took him prisoner – to know that they approve his will. I do not yet know the answer.

The suspension of hostilities lasted until nine o'clock. Then the English saluted us with 12 cannon rounds. The same day we noticed that the English had set fire to their entrenchment at the *Sault*, and the fire reignited at the houses of *Petit-Pré*.

25 – The English started firing their from their battery on *Pointe de Lévy*, and killed two men on the rampart.

26 – The English fire continues.

27 – It was decided that *Sieurs Duel* and *La Garenne*, commanding the *Domaine* battery, and *M. Levasseur* would go with the elite men to arm the six frigates anchored in *Batiscan. M. Cadet*,[78] at the head, embarked everyone that same day, leaving in the *chaloupe*.[79] *M. de Bougainville* was to leave with 2,000 men to march south, toward St Antoine, to beat the enemy.

The *chaloupe* set off indiscreetly, in sight of the enemy, who cannonaded the boats without causing damage. They returned the same night to *Pointe aux Trembles.*

The same evening the enemy, undoubtedly informed of our approach, were favored at nine o'clock in the evening with a light north-east wind, and passed with a frigate of 28 guns, a ship of 18, one of 8, one of 6 and one of 4. We noticed that our batteries were thinned, for the fire was not lively; they passed, I believe, without receiving much harm.

The English batteries rained hellfire from *Pointe de Lévy*, both in bombs and shot. A man beside me on the ramparts was killed, by a cannonball which passed through the walls of the battery; 3 men were killed at the *Dauphine* battery of

76 *Petit Pré*: on the north shore of the northern channel of the Rivière St Laurent as it passes Isle d'Orléans, just north of l'Ange Gardien. *Château* Richer is just north of Petit Pré on the northern shoreline.

77 *Ochterlony*: see footnote 90, p.46. *De St Laurent*: see footnote 92, p.47. Other versions of the story have the French soldier serving in the Guyenne Regiment; Panet uses 'Languedoc'.

78 *Joseph-Michel Cadet*: see footnote 6, p.72.

79 *Chaloupe*: footnote 58, p.28.

M. Gareu, and 15 wounded and burned by *gargousses* that caught fire on the old battery.[80]

It is to be observed that the English vessels anchored at *Écureuils* descended to *Cap Rouge* and to *Pointe aux Trembles*.[81]

That same night we feared a landing; in fact, we were warned they had discovered barges at *l'Anse des Mères*. We received a reinforcement from the camp below *Beauport*, composed of 4 pickets of regular troops, of 50 men each, and of 50 grenadiers. *M. de Bernetz*, commander there, had them posted, namely: a picket in the lower town, at the [*Batterie*] *Construction*, one at *l'Anse des Mères*, another at *Samos*, and the one at *Sillery* with the grenadiers, to oppose the landing.[82]

28 August – Our alarm had no results. While following orders and returning his troops to *Jacques Cartier*, *Courval*,[83] who commands the frigate *Bienfaisant*,[84] was wounded dangerously in the thigh by a Canadian who was in the woods and who, being afraid, shot at him. He unfortunately had a uniform like an Englishman; we fear he will not survive.

29 – In the morning, a continuation of the cannonade and bombardment of *Pointe de Lévy*.

30 – The English ships that were in front of *St Augustin* and *Cape Rouge* fired a considerable cannonade from one until eight o'clock in the morning. At 5 a.m. they attempted a landing with flat bottomed boats near *St Augustin*. 40 sailors from *M. Denet*'s boats, who had thrown themselves ashore, having abandoned their boats, fired from the woods. This firing brought the first reinforcements to this area, and the enemy re-embarked. We had a Canadian man killed, and one wounded. We do not know the enemy losses, as they are not landed.

31 – All morning the English laid considerable cannonfire from *Pointe de Lévy*. The same day, at 9 o'clock in the evening, 7 vessels passed, including a frigate of 20 guns, and 6 vessels, schooners or boats, despite the fire of our batteries, which pierced several.

1 September – The English continued to burn their entrenchments at the *Sault*, and continued to shell and bombard the city. Their focus was on the neighborhood of *St Roch*.

80 *Gargousse*: see footnote 55, p.84.
81 *Cap Rouge*: see footnote 54, p.26.
82 *Félicien de Bernetz*: see footnote 67, p.31.
83 *François-Louis Poulin de Courval*: see footnote 59, p.29.
84 *Bienfaisant*; see footnote 111, p.55. Panet uses 'Brassavran'.

2 – At ten o'clock in the morning we saw considerable movement on the part of the enemy: three big English ships heading from the *Cap* to just north-east of the city, were anchored between the tip of the island and *Pointe de Lévy*. We clearly see about 40 barges loaded with people, between these vessels, keeping abreast. This movement put the city on the alert; I went, after drinking two shots at *Magnan*'s at *Porte St Jean*, and we drank the third to the alarm.[85] We went to *Porte St Louis*, where the commander was, who, having seen the maneuver, assigned me gladly to the *St Louis Battery*; from here I discovered that the barges were returning to *Pointe de Lévy*; that there were 40 others who followed the north channel, going to *Isle d'Orléans*.

3 – 17 English vessels, including a large ship of 60 guns, 3 frigates and other vessels were anchored from *Cap Rouge* to *Sillery*. They formed a 'C' to close the entrance to the *Rivière Cap Rouge*. This movement sped up the arrival of *M. Bougainville*; we detached about 500 men to guard this front. On the same day 3 men were killed, including two at *M. Dunet*'s battery, and one on the ramparts, by the firing from *Pointe de Lévy*.

4 – It was noticed at the *Beauport* camp that the enemy had completely evacuated the fort. That there remained only two small vessels anchored opposite the church at *l'Ange Gardien*.

The same day, they sent a scout to the *Sault*; we discovered no English; the inhabitants found their wheat in good condition, and less damaged than those near our soldiers.

An order was given to set fire to three entrenchments that the English had not burned, which was executed in the morning. 4 barges appeared at *Samos*, which withdrew at the first discharge.

We have learned, and do not know if it is true, from an English engineer, taken by *Dufy*,[86] and 5 other soldiers and 3 savages, that General Amherst did not intend to advance further; it was risking your life to bring this news to General Wolfe. This engineer reports that the news is that we are masters of the best part of Ireland; I wish it were [so].

6 – The English began a considerable fire from *Pointe de Lévy*, and dismounted a battery of the po [...] they made [...].

The same day, being at *M. Dunet*'s the battery, someone came to warn us that above the *Côte de Begin*, on the Main Road, he passed a column of English troops.[87] *Sieur Gareau* and *Dunet* each pointed a cannon of 24 pounds, that they charged

85 *Porte St Jean*: on Rue St Jean, facing west toward St Foi.

86 Most likely Dufils Charest: see footnote 61, p.29.

87 *Côte de Begin*: I have not found a definitive source for a location by this name, or an alternate name.

with a load and half. The first blow landed in the column and must have inconvenienced some more than they expected, because the shot carried so far; the second shot went over the column, forcing a move that leads us to think that the first shot had inconvenienced them.

The same day, at 8 o'clock, there was an alarm. *M. de Bougainville*, who was at *St Augustin*, had seen the English parade along the *Etchemins* River; then he had seen them return. We sent 5 pickets from various regiments with a company of grenadiers. I went to *Porte St Louis*, but there was nothing new.

7 – All the English vessels headed toward *Sillery*. They made different movements to the south, which worried us.

The battery at *Pointe de Lévy* kept up a continual fire, which killed an ensign at *M. Dunet*'s battery, and one wounded.

A small schooner of about 40 tons passed in front of the city at three o'clock, on a light north-west wind. We imagined it was a dare because there were only about 15 men, 8 of whom appeared to be officers, steadying themselves and completing the maneuver. They succeeded in their challenge, since most of the officers held to their bridge. We fired about 100 rounds which, showing our esteem, only pierced their sails.

8 – The English have hardly fired in front of the city. The Canadians sent to the north country reported that everything was burned, with the exception of the churches, and no harm to the crops.

The same day, a deserter swam from *Isle d'Orléans*; he is rather connected with the first.

(The rest of the manuscript has not been preserved.)

3

Gilles-Armand Joannès

Gilles-Armand Joannès (some records use Égide-Armand) was born in Belfort, France, on 24 February 1735 and died in *Porrentruy*, Switzerland, on 14 January 1814. In a 1967 article for the *Archivum Heraldicum: International Bulletin*,[1] Robert Genevoy states: 'Along the outer walls of the chapel St Germain in Porrentruy have been mounted tombstones and memorials from the old cemetery which surrounded the church. Among these memories of the past, a monument commemorates the death of Gilles-Armand de Joannès, former Maréchal de Camp.'[2]

Joannès enlisted as a *lieutenant* in the Languedoc Regiment on 17 March 1747, at the age of 12, and progressed steadily up the ranks to captain in 1755. Genevoy states that Gilles-François Joannès, his father, was employed as the King's Engineer in Belfort. His son would follow in his footsteps, assigned as the engineer of Québec from 1757 to 1759. Comte Maurès de Malartic's journal entry for 2 August 1759 indicates troops were sent to Sillery as workmen 'under the direction of M. Joannès, major of Languedoc.'

During the 1759 siege of Québec Joannès would also act as interpreter and emissary between Jean-Baptiste-Nicolas-Roch de Ramezay, French commander in Québec City, and Brigadier General George Townshend, third in the line of British command for the expedition, and unexpected commander following the death of Major General James Wolfe and the wounding of Brigadier General Robert Monckton on the fateful 13 September. On the recommendation of the Duc de Lévis, Joannès was made a Chevalier de St Louis on 12 September 1769, and he received his final promotion to *maréchal de camp* on 20 October 1790. Genevoy indicates that at this time Joannès was the *lieutenant colonel* of the Provincial Regiment of Paris. Gilles-Armand Joannès emigrated to Porrentruy in 1791 and remained there until his death in 1814.

1 Robert Genevoy, 'Armoiries Joannès et Michel de Boucherolles au cimetière Saint Germain de Porrentruy', *Archivum Heraldicum International* Bulletin 41:1(1967), https://www.e-periodica.ch/digbib/view?pid=ahe-002:1967:81::4#44 (accessed 13 June 2019), p.40.

2 In the same article Genevoy indicates that although the tombstone reads 'Gilles-Armand de Joannès', his recorded name at birth is simply 'Gilles-Armand Joannès'.

Memoir of the 1759 Campaign from the month of May until September by M. Joannès, Major of Québec[3]

In the fear of the enemy which gripped us on the northern frontiers of the colony, the *Marquis de Vaudreuil* sent *M. de Bourlamaque*,[4] brigadier, with the *La Reine* battalion, two of *Berry* and a body of 1,000 to 1,200 Canadians, to head to *Carillon* in the first days of May. This officer had orders to put the fort in its best possible state, and to work at repairing the entrenchments which had been raised the year before, while having secret orders that, at the approach of the enemy, he was to evacuate and blow up this fort, as well as *St Frédéric*, and withdraw to *Isle aux Noix*, at the entrance of Lake Champlain, a position recognized in the spring by the *Chevalier de Lévis* which would assure the communication of supplies for this frontier and enable this party to be reinforced more efficiently, if the enemy presented itself in force, as it was closer to the interior of the colony.[5]

At the same time, the *Marquis de Vaudreuil* sent *M. Pouchot*, captain in the *Béarn* regiment,[6] with three picquets of Colony troops and a body of 8 to 900 savages and Canadians to capture Niagara, a post that covered our border along the shores of Lake Ontario. This officer had an order from the *Marquis de Vaudreuil* to pass on to *M. de Lignery*,[7] captain of the Colony troops, the body of savages and Canadians he took with him, in the event that the enemy does not seem prepared to contest his arrival at Niagara; and *M. de Lignery* has orders, for his part, to march with his men and any which he had brought back from the evacuation of *Fort Duquesne*, to reclaim this post from the enemy. The *Marquis de Montcalm* was strongly opposed to this plan aimed at taking back *Belle Rivière*;[8] his plan being to reduce our defensive forces as much as possible, and to draw the frontiers in closer to the center of the colony; but in considering the likely interruption to the fur trade, his opinion was not followed.

The area around *Québec* is the only one neglected. The enemy, who since the beginning of this war, had threatened it [the city], and whose operations had always been delayed, the difficulties in crossing a river that had always been regarded as impracticable without the help of coastal pilots, who do not pass some places in this river without trembling, and still more the shipwrecks that the English had

3 This translation has been prepared from Doughty and Parmelee, *The Siege of Quebec*, vol.4, p.219.

4 François-Charles de Bourlamaque: see footnote 82, p.38.

5 François-Gaston de Lévis, Duc de Lévis: see footnote 28, p.20.

6 Pierre Pouchot: see footnote 83, p.38.

7 *François-Marie le Marchand de Lignery*: see footnote 100, p.49.

8 *Belle Rivière*: 180–200 km NNW of Québec City, and SSE of *Lac St Jean*. Used as a general term for the area along the river, which in turn takes its name from its source, *Lac de la Belle Rivière*.

left on the *Isle aux Oeufs*, in their last advance on *Québec*, increased the confidence and security for this frontier.[9]

The *Marquis de Montcalm*, however, as well as *M. Pontleroy*, chief engineer in Canada,[10] had given several proposals to *M.* the *Marquis de Vaudreuil* to strengthen this area, by a chain of proposed redoubts along the *Beauport* coast, the easiest place to stage a landing, to put *Québec* in a state of defense; but this is not the only occasion where their views were ignored. In the end, this was the state of things when *M. de Bougainville* arrived on May 14th with two King's frigates and a small fleet of about 18 ships loaded with supplies of munitions and food.[11] This officer, familiar with the considerable arming of the English and their intention to attack the capital, raised alarms upon arriving; the *Marquis de Montcalm* immediately left *Montréal* to prepare as much as was possible; the *Marquis de Vaudreuil* followed him a few days later; and the *Chevalier de Lévis* remained in *Montréal*, as well as the troops quartered there, who were being delayed as much as possible before being sent on campaign, in order to save supplies, the soldiers having been boarded with the inhabitants during the winter. This general was able to go to the different frontiers where the enemy seemed to be the nearest.

On May 24th it was announced that the enemy, on board 13 large vessels, appeared at *St Barnabé*,[12] 60 leagues below *Québec*. The *Chevalier de Lévis* received an order to immediately go there with the 5 battalions still in quarters. The militias of three parishes were also ordered to assemble, and they held a council of war to determine the measures to be taken for the defense of the colony. They settled on making several fireships of the little fleet which had arrived in the spring; the construction of a number of rafts was ordered, and finally they prepared small *bâteaux*, mounting a cannon on the front, and built a floating battery of 12 cannons. At the mouth of the *Rivière St Charles* they grounded two old naval vessels as batteries. This was the plan to defend the river. The plan for the ground defense was to prevent a landing by the enemy. *Québec*, whose open approaches were defended with simple palisades, was considered indefensible, was only occupied as a post to the right of our army that is extended from this place to the stream at *Beauport*, which was fordable in several places and easily access; this led the *Chevalier de Lévis* to oppose leaving the left of the army this poorly secured; and it was on his reiterated insistences that it was decided to extend to the *Rivière Montmorency*, as being more considerable and easier to defend.

9 *Ile-aux-Oeufs*: an islet in the Rivière St Laurent 400 km NE of Québec City and tight to the northern shore of the river. Home for many varieties of nesting birds, the island also has dangerous reefs which, in 1690 and 1711, ended British expeditions to take Québec.

10 *Nicolas Sarrebource de Pontleroy*: see footnote 37, p.22.

11 Bougainville arrived from France with this flotilla from Bordeaux [note added by the editor of the 1910 edition].

12 *Isle St Barnabé*: see footnote 16, p.73.

M. de Bougainville received orders to immediately establish a camp at *Beauport* with the grenadiers and a number of Canadians, to start work along this shore, the *Marquis de Vaudreuil* having also sent several of the Colony troops, with orders to evacuate the houses down along the river and to hide, a few leagues into woods, women, children and livestock; but the enemy, who they discovered for the most part did not miss [had not gone without] beef during the whole campaign, which made us believe needlessly enough that horses had been fed to the troops all winter. The whole month of June was spent on our part entrenching and putting us in a position to await the enemy; during this time 2 or 300 savages joined us.

The English ships, however, arrived successively in the river; and finally on the 27th of this month they landed a body of troops on *Isle d'Orléans*. The savages and Canadians who had been sent to harass them returned with having taken only a few scalps. The 29th, the enemy landed troops at *Beaumont*, surprising the officer commanding several light troops; this officer, forced to flee, left the orders he had from the *Marquis de Vaudreuil* to evacuate the houses, which provided the enemy with available places to live.

On the 30th the enemy appeared at *Pointe de Lévy*; we sent some savages to worry them in their camp. The *Marquis de Montcalm*'s plan was to pass, during the night, a body to dislodge them; but one of their deserters having assured the General that he would be attacked the same night, he cancelled the project; however, on the 28th they [the French] released the fireships; but, by either terror or inability of those who commanded them, they produced no effect, the fire having been started more than a league from the English fleet, which had anchored the day before within view of our camp.

The enemy, masters of *Pointe de Lévy*, worked immediately to entrench and at the same time establish a battery of large guns and mortars near their camp, which being finished on the 12th of July, did not stop firing, day or night, balls, bombs, *carcasses* and fire-pots, until the 18th of September.[13] During this time, the fire has reduced more than 240 of the most beautiful houses to ashes, ruin upsets and crushes the rest of this unfortunate city.

The *Marquis de Montcalm* had not thought it appropriate to thin out his front, which was already too extended for his strength, and could have left some places too weak; however, after repeated requests from the Canadians who foresaw, by the establishment of this battery, the ruin of the city, and who wanted to take sole charge of this operation, he sent a body of about 1,500 Canadians, taken by preference over the citizens of the city as the interested parties, and added 60 regulars. But this detachment, having passed under cover of darkness to the opposite side of *Québec*, was not yet in range of the enemy when a terror spread among the militiamen; some gunshots were fired, three or four men were wounded; they feared discovery and returned to the square without having done anything.

13 *Carcasses*: footnote 68, p.31.

The enemy, however, who from their camp on *Pointe de Lévy* judged our position too advantageous and wanting to remove us by force, passed a body of troops to the left bank of *Rivière Montmorency* and there build a battery of 50 large artillery guns, in hopes of forcing our left, whom they faced on the right bank of the same river, to withdraw. The *Chevalier de Lévis*, who commanded in this area as far as the brook at *Beauport*, contented himself in pulling back the camp and cutting traverses under fire of the batteries, and at the same time placing the guard in trenches. It is with the help of these batteries and 2 ships mounting 16 guns each, that they had grounded at high tide; and a big ship of 74 guns that they had embossed,[14] that they tried on July 31st to force us from these parts. The engagement was begun at eleven in the morning by a brisk bombardment from their ships and their batteries, whose fire was crossing. The *Chevalier de Lévis* took command of the left wing and notified the *Marquises de Vaudreuil* and *Montcalm*, who immediately reinforced the line with the grenadier companies and the *Guyenne* regiment; the latter general took the remaining troops to the place the enemy would likely attack. At four o'clock in the evening, the body that was camped on *Pointe de Lévy* appeared in rowboats, while those camped at *Sault Montmorency* appeared in column on the left bank of this river, which can be forded at its mouth during low tide. They attacked jointly with the troops that had dismounted on the exposed sea flats, and headed for a redoubt which had been evacuated; but the superior fire of our entrenchments forced them to abandon it, after having lost in this action 7 to 800 of their best troops, both killed or wounded, having kept us under fire for seven hours from over 80 pieces of artillery.

On the 18th of this month the enemy had passed 7 ships of various sizes above *Québec*; which made it easy for them to land light troops who captured several women and cattle. We immediately sent *M. Dumas*,[15] a major of Colony troops, with about 1,000 to 1,200 men, Canadians or savages, who, after having forced the enemy to re-embark, remained there to observe the movements of these 7 ships, which left us jealous for our food.

In the first days of August we received news that *M. de Bourlamaque* had evacuated fort *Carillon* as well as *St Frédéric*, in accordance with the instruction he had received, at the approach of *Général* Amherst (after, however, having blown up these two places). We also learned that *M. Pouchot*, *commandant* at Niagara, had capitulated after twenty-two days under siege, and after the troops of *M. de Lignery* coming to his aid had been beaten.

On August 10th, the colony finding itself open and undefended on this frontier, the *Marquis de Vaudreuil* ordered the *Chevalier de Lévis* to take command of a body of troops going above the rapids of the Rivière St Laurent and scout a

14 A ship is embossed when it is secured in a specific position through the use of two mooring lines, front and rear.

15 *Jean-Daniel Dumas*: see footnote 75, p.35.

position to be fortified, in order to oppose the efforts of the enemy army after the capture of Niagara.

The enemy came up again during the night, and moved several ships above *Québec* during the ebb tide; we immediately sent *M. de Bougainville* with some troops to take command of the force which had been commanded by *M. Dumas.* On the eighth the enemy appeared 7 leagues above Québec, numbering about 1,500 men. *M. de Bougainville*, who had followed them the moment they set foot on ground, forced them to re-embark. The evening on this same day, the same body which had benefited from the falling tide tried to make a second landing a little lower; but *M. de Bougainville* also forced them to push their boats off before they could put everyone ashore.

The rest of the month of August passed in a fierce bombardment from the enemy, both on the left of our army and on the city; *carcasses* and fire-pots ignited several parts of the city. Finally, September 3rd, the enemy, after having ruined, devastated, burned and ravaged all the dwellings from *Québec* to the river bottom, abandoned the camp they had on the left bank of the *Rivière Montmorency*, and returned to the camp they had previously occupied on the *Pointe de Lévy.*

During the whole month of August the savages attacked the enemy, each time we had the chance, and where just the same we could not kill them all, mainly on the 10th and the 15th of June, that the enemies tried to force the fords guarded by *M. de Repentigny* and the savages. But the enemy, having landed with some light troops 14 leagues above *Québec*, burned a house holding all the equipment for the officers of the five army battalions, who had been ordered to send them there, keeping only one tent for two officers and one very small case. *M. de Bougainville*, who followed them along the riverbank, could not arrive in time to prevent them from landing; he forced them to re-embark and even took some prisoners from their rear guard. On September 4th, the enemy troops who had left the camp at the *Sault de Montmorency* marched above *Québec*, on the right bank of the river, to embark on the fleet which they had there. The *Marquis de Montcalm* thought it was necessary to strengthen *M. de Bougainville*'s corps of grenadier companies, one picquet per battalion, and the volunteers from Canadian troops, which formed a body of about 2,300 to 2,400 men. This body, assigned to cover, from *Québec* to 7 leagues or more above it, the left bank of the river, was divided into several picquets which occupied the best points along this shore for making a landing, and the rest following along beside the enemy and observing their movements. The enemy, attentive to our maneuvers, intended nothing more than tiring the body that was watching them; that is why, with the help of the tide, it was six leagues and more above *Québec*, and at low tide had arrived just a quarter of a league from this city. The body covering them followed their movements exactly, with great difficulty and an extraordinary effort. Finally, having managed to exhaust them, they held them in check 3 leagues above *Québec*, the night of the 12th to 13th, by the 20 ships that they had there, and took advantage of the darkness to land their troops, who, helped by the falling tide and a strong wind coming down the river, came to land during the same night about half a league from *Québec*, where they attacked and established a post. *M. de Bougainville* was only informed of the enemy landing by deserters, the ships having kept him distracted, feigning to disembark. He marched immediately, but unfortunately arrived only after the affair was decided against us.

The enemy, however, having succeeded in the landing, immediately formed up; the city and the army were warned of the enemy landing by the gunshots from the post which the enemy attacked, and the *Chevalier de Bernetz*,[16] a retired lieutenant colonel of the *Royal Roussillon*, who had been in command for more than a month in the absence of *M. de Ramezay*, brought out some local militia to harass the enemy. The *Guyenne* regiment, which was on the right and had been reinforced at the expense of the left wing, when the position was determined to be less critical since the abandonment of the camp that the enemy had there, went immediately beside the city of *Québec*; but finding the enemy too numerous, he [Bernetz] contented extending his front to make an appearance and to give the army time to reach the battlefield. The *Marquis de Montcalm* marched to the field, leaving, however, the *Marquis de Vaudreuil* with a lieutenant colonel and 1,500 men in the different posts of the camp. The *Marquis de Montcalm* formed his troops as they arrived. He had on his right a thicket of small woods which stretched forward; on his left, the country, cut by some mounds and scrub, determined that these two terrains were more appropriate for the Canadians; he put 1,500 on his right and the rest on his left; he placed the 5 battalions of regular troops in the center with platoons of Canadians in advance, hiding behind some banks. We fired for a long time; finally, the *Marquis de Montcalm*, seeing the enemy force grow more and more numerous, and some cannon firing, decided not to give them time to become stronger; he gave the signal to charge the enemy. Troops shook with a fervor, as well as the Canadians, but after a few steps forward, the small patch of woods that stretched to the right served as a retreat for the Canadians, who left the five battalions to walk alone; the advanced platoons barely had time to retreat from their positions and to rejoin their units, which caused a bit of hesitation; finally, after having come within a pistol's range, and having fired three or four discharges, the right folded and dragged along the rest of line. The *Marquis de Montcalm*, who had been mortally wounded, returned to the city where he died of his wounds. The Canadians, however, which were withdrawn on the right, and which, by their movement, had caused the disorder in the line, were forced out of their scrub, and this is where some of them were killed or taken prisoner.

The *Marquis de Vaudreuil*, who had remained as he was told at the camp, judged by the great musket fire that the affair was begun, went there; but on the road he met the army returning in disorder to his camp. On that he assembled a war council, in which it was judged necessary to leave the *Beauport* camp, whose communication to food supplies was cut off by the position of the enemy army, and to retire to *Jacques Cartier*.

16 *Félicien de Bernetz*: see footnote 67, p.31. Joannès uses 'Bernets'.

It is necessary to point out that they had carried the cargoes arrived from France up to 18 leagues above *Québec*, to protect them from being burned by the enemy; and it is to this place they would go, as the destruction went on, for the provisions necessary for the army.

On September 13th, the same day he vacated the camp, the *Marquis de Vaudreuil* sent an instruction to *M. de Ramezay*.[17] On the 15th, this commander, who remained in his place on the day of the action, assembled a war council where it was decided, on the assurances he gave, that by the accounts which were made and by the careful research he had done among the different individuals, that there was only food for three or four days at most; besides without hope of relief for the army, of which there had been no news since the affair, it was, I report, decided to surrender to the most honorable conditions for the King's arms.

The communication with the army not being broken, I suggested to send out an elite detachment from the garrison to join the army, but I was the only one of my opinion. The enemy profited from these two days by entrenching themselves in their new position and starting work on batteries about 300 *toises* from the center of the place.[18]

On the 16th of this month, a cavalry detachment that was seen at the former camp at *Beauport* gave us a voice for hope of assistance, both in food and in troops; for the garrison of *Québec*, too few in number for its defenses, composed for the most part of militia and sailors, could not protect this place from a sudden attack.

I was dispatched to the *Marquis de Vaudreuil* by *M. de Ramezay* to press for this help, after demanding from me my word of honor to be back in the same night; but having learned 3 leagues along the way, with certainty, that the *Marquis de Vaudreuil* was himself 10 or 12 leagues distant, I did not think I could go and return in the time that had been prescribed to me. That is why I decided to write to the *Marquis de Vaudreuil* and send him my letter by an artillery horseman with the order to deliver it to *M. de Bougainville*, who had positioned his troops 3 leagues from *Québec* to collect the debris and the stragglers of the army. The latter wrote to *M. de Ramezay* in reply, and indicated to him places in *Québec* where he could find flour from different individuals. *M. de Ramezay* had also received, after my departure, a letter from *M. de Vaudreuil* these two letters offering him help, which he communicated to no one, changing nothing in the decision he had made to capitulate, and it is only on the journey that I made to the army after the capitulation that I have learned the contents. Returning, however, to the city on the evening of the 16th, I reported to the *commandant* about the letter I had written to the *Marquis de Vaudreuil*, in which I told him about the critical situation of the place, and the resolution to capitulate on the 17th, if the assistance did not appear by ten o'clock in the morning, but perhaps we could delay until evening.

17 King's Lieutenant in Québec, that is to say *commandant* of Québec [note added by the editor of the 1910 edition].

18 *Toises*: see footnote 13, p.17.

The 17th day, when I learned that *M. de Ramezay* had received the two letters above without having communicated them, and on the order he gave me to be ready to go at ten o'clock in the morning to propose the capitulation, I protested to everyone the recommendation I had given to the war council, as things looked different; and I proposed to perform more thorough searches for flour myself; we therefore did not speak more of capitulation until four o'clock in the evening; but in this time the enemy having maneuvered their big ships, pretending to emboss six in front of the lower town, the [truce] flag was raised on the shore of the harbor and on the land. I tore them down, not believing that we had changed our opinion; but at once I received a written order to surrender, and the notice was handed to me accordingly. I had, however, heard the *Marquis de Vaudreuil* would not arrive to help until evening; so I tried to create difficulties to draw things out, holding on to what little power I possessed when leaving *Québec*; I delayed until eleven o'clock in the evening, at which time the English general required me to have the answer. I went back to the city and gave account to *M. de Ramezay* of the difficulties I had encountered; but I received a second order in writing to return at eleven o'clock in the evening, help not yet having appeared in this time. M. *de la Roche-Beaucourt*,[19] commanding the cavalry troop, entered shortly after my departure for the capitulation, which I had orders to finish, with 60 horses, each carrying a bag of biscuit and promising help.

The presence of the *Chevalier de Lévis*, who had just rejoined the army, had revived the confidence and courage of the troops. He had inspired feelings of vigor which gave him the hope of rescuing the place, and indeed he marched forward and sent *M. de Bougainville* to throw himself into *Québec* with some elite troops. *M. de Ramezay* did not think it desirable to break the capitulation, which had been started, which was to be signed the following day, the 18th. This *commandant*, who feared perhaps to be taken by force, might have, as had been proposed by *M. de Fredmont*, an artillery officer, and by myself, abandon the lower town separated from the upper by ditches, and to reinforce, by the troops that it would have drawn to the upper town, which is unmanned in many parts due to its vast circumference. This officer, who has never seen war in a wilderness, did not know how to defend a post. It is at least necessary to presume, as he did not accept this advice, that he buttressed himself on the orders he had from the *Marquis de Vaudreuil* not to risk taking sword in hand.

It is true that most of the militia and sailors composing the garrison of *Québec* were of the worst will. The bad mien that the officers of these troops held was taking me to the point of falling upon two of these officers with sword-blows. They threatened nothing less than giving up their posts and abandoning their troops. We can judge by that their bad disposition. Several had already run and deserted.

The Journal abruptly ends at this point.

19 Aide-de-camp of the Marquis de Montcalm [note added by the editor of the 1910 edition].

4

Marie-Joseph Legardeur de Repentigny, Sœur de la Visitation

The final memoir has been taken from the 1858 English-language publication *The Siege of Quebec in 1759*, printed by the Mercury Office in Québec, 'First published, in French, by the Literary and Historical Society of Quebec' in 1840. Unsigned and unattributed at the time of its publication, it is now widely accepted as the work of Marie-Joseph Legardeur de Repentigny, Sœur de la Visitation, *supérieure* at the General Hospital in Québec.

In 1693, the General Hospital opened in Québec, founded by Monsignor Jean-Baptiste de La Croix de Chevrières de Saint-Vallier to serve the poor, sick and needy inhabitants of the city. Care was provided by Augustinian nuns who had trained and served at the city's other hospital, the *Hôtel Dieu*. In 1721 the General Hospital and the area surrounding it became the parish of Notre Dame des Anges.[1]

Among the community of nuns to serve at the General Hospital was Marie-Joseph Legardeur de Repentigny, born at Montréal in 1693, daughter of Pierre Legardeur de Repentigny and Agathe de Saint-Père. Her uncle, Augustin Legardeur de Courtemanche,[2] and an aunt, Marie-Joseph Leneuf de la Vallière, were godparents. Her father, the *Sieur* de Bourdon, was primarily a soldier who progressed slowly but regularly through the ranks of the militia and Colony troops. Described as indolent and rather easy-going, Pierre was sometimes overshadowed by his

1 Jean Simard, 'The Augustinian Monastery of Quebec', *Encyclopedia of French Cultural Heritage in North America* (Québec: Société Héritage de Champlain, 2008–), http://www.ameriquefrancaise.org/en/article-570/The_Augustinian_Monastery_of_Quebec.html (accessed 29 October 2018).

2 Augustin Legardeur de Courtemanche (1663–1717): soldier, ambassador, *commandant* at Labrador. *Enseigne* 1690; half-pay *lieutenant* 1691, *lieutenant* 1692, and commanding a company by 1702. In 1700 he was involved in attempts to negotiate a peace between the Ottawas and the Iroquois. Nora T. Corley, 'Legardeur de Courtemanche, Augustin', in *Dictionary of Canadian Biography*, vol.2 (Toronto: University of Toronto/Université Laval, 2003–).

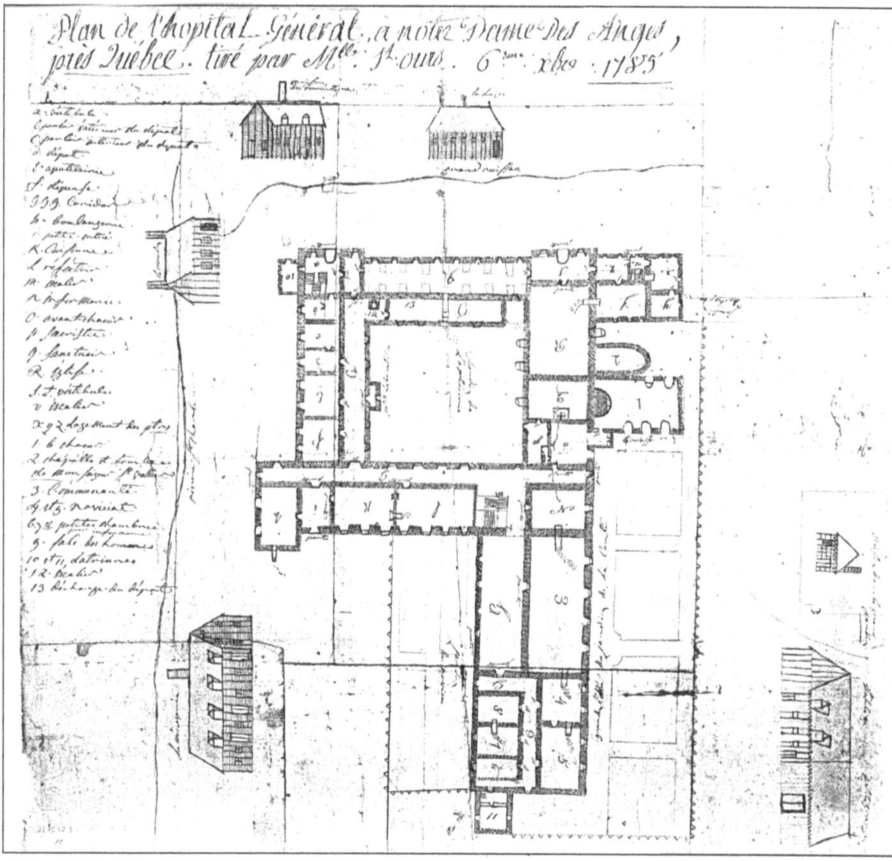

Plan of the ground floor of the *Hôpital Général* at Notre-Dame-des-Anges near Québec, Mademoiselle Saint-Ours, 6 October 1785 (Monastère des Augustines de l'Hôpital Général de Québec fonds. HG-A-23.15.12.1)

wife.[3] Agathe de Saint-Père was a talented businesswoman, starting out in the sale and marketing of maple syrup, as well as in developing techniques for making fabrics with local products. In 1705 she opened her first factory of 'paintings, druggists, serges, crosses and *couverces* [covers].'[4]

3 Paul-André Dubé, 'Legardeur de Repentigny, Pierre (1657–1736)', in *Dictionary of Canadian Biography*, vol.2 (Toronto: University of Toronto/Université Laval, 2003–).

4 The biographical information for Marie-Joseph Legardeur de Repentigny for this introduction comes from a single source and will be footnoted only once. In it, author Julie Roy made what I found to be a most important point regarding this *mémoire*: it is the first truly Canadian telling of the story. Julie Roy, 'Marie-Joseph Legardeur de Repentigny, *mère supérieure hospitalière* (Canada, 1693 – Canada, 1776)',

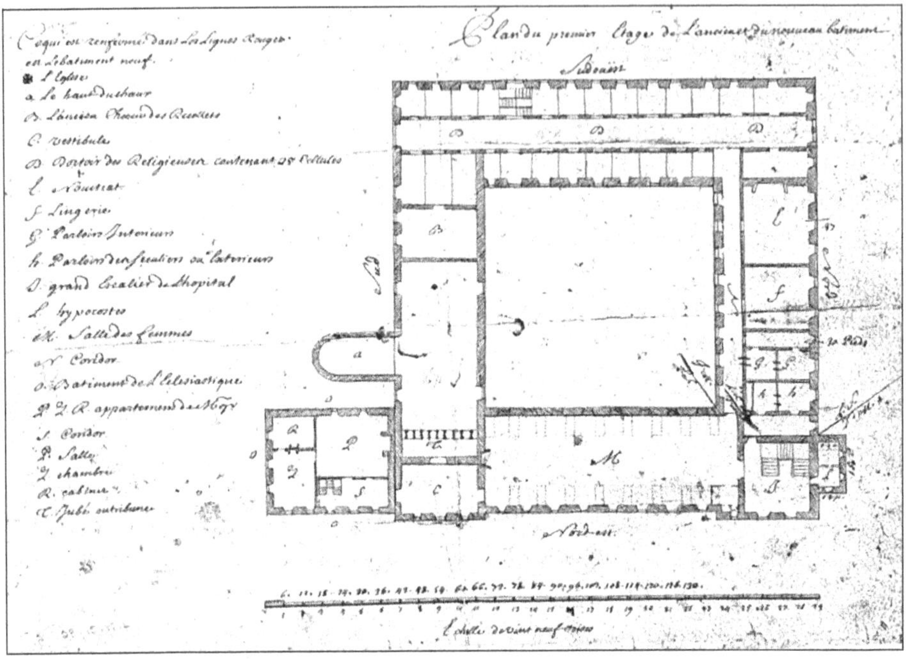

Plan of the first floor of the old and new building, 18th Century (Monastère des Augustines de l'Hôpital général de Québec fonds. HG-A-23.15.12.6)

Marie-Joseph was educated at the Congrégation Notre-Dame de Montréal, before becoming a resident with the Ursulines of Québec. In 1715 she dedicated herself to a religious life, hoping to serve the poor and those in need at the General Hospital. The community there was only allowed to have 12 members, and they were already fully staffed. That did not stop Marie-Joseph. She started her training at the *Hôtel Dieu*, beginning her novitiate in the fall of 1715. At the same time she used her connections with the Marquis de Vaudreuil and Monsignor de Saint-Vallier to press for a position at the General Hospital. On 22 March 1718, after new openings were created, Marie-Joseph joined the hospital, and finalized her vows on 30 May as *Sœur de la Visitation*. In 1725 a boarding school was added to the Augustinian faculties, and Marie-Joseph began a 10-year period overseeing the young students. Always short on finances, the hospital began caring for invalided soldiers in 1727, the beginning of their time as a military hospital.

In April of 1747 Sœur de la Visitation was elected *mère supérieure* for a term of three years, after which she served as an assistant to the new *supérieure*,

in Gaston Deschênes and Denis Vaugeois (eds.), *Vivre la Conquête*, vol.2 (Lille: Septentrion, 2014), pp.148–157.

Marie-Joseph Juchereau-Duchesnay, who had taken the name Mother of the Child Jesus. In November 1759 Marie-Joseph would again assume the role of *supérieure*. Throughout her time as *supérieure*, Sœur de la Visitation was faced with severe financial strain caused by the war and France's failure to repay the Augustinians' considerable expenditures for the care and feeding of French citizens and soldiers who had come to them for assistance during the siege. No fewer than 600 people had taken refuge in the hospital, including wounded soldiers from both armies.

General Murray, the British governor in Québec, was very quick to reimburse the order for the expenses incurred caring for the British sick and wounded. The same cannot be said for the French court. In 1763 Marie-Joseph wrote to the Minister of the King's Court in France, asking for immediate reimbursement for services rendered during the war. The letter received no reply. By 1765 the monastery and hospital were at risk of default and foreclosure by its creditors. Marie-Joseph used the format of a letter to her fellow Augustinians, seemingly as part of the order's instruction to share information and updates with sister communities, but more than likely a move designed to bring knowledge of the hospital's peril to those outside the French Court and seek their assistance in securing payment. In so doing she created the memoir which follows. In it she includes a detailed account of the events, the deprivations suffered by the inhabitants, and the limits to which the Augustinian Sisters extended themselves in caring for the community and soldiers.

Sœur de la Visitation, Marie-Joseph Legardeur de Repentigny, would remain in her position as *supérieure* until 1766, at the age of 73, when she returned to her role as an advisor. In 1768 the order would finally receive reimbursement from the King's Court in France, but only one-fifth of that which they had expended. Marie-Joseph died at the age of 82, on 10 June 1776.

Siege of Québec
In
1759

NARRATIVE of the doings during the Siege of Québec, and the conquest of Canada; by a nun of the General Hospital of Québec, transmitted to a religious community of the same order, in France.

My Very Reverend Mothers,
As our constitution requires us to consult the other establishments of our Congregation, in any difficulties that may occur, tending to impede the progress of our holy Institution, it must also give you the same power, I imagine, when necessary to promote our edification. The simple narration, which I am about to give you, of what passed since the year 1755, when the English determined to use every effort to acquire this colony; the part we took, by the immense labors which were consequently imposed upon us, will be the subject.

The General Hospital is situated in the outer limits of Québec, about half a mile from the walls.

The fire,[5] from which our Sisters in Québec have lately suffered, having rendered it impossible for them to continue their charge of the sick, Mr Bigot, the Intendant[6] of the country, proposed that we should receive them in our hospital. We readily agreed so to do; being desirous of rendering service, and zealously fulfilling the duties of our calling, the Sisters lost no time in entering upon the sacred work. His Majesty, attentive to the wants of his subjects, and being informed of the preparations making by the English, did not fail to forward succor to the country, consisting in numerous vessels, laden with munitions of war and provisions, of which we were entirely destitute; and several regiments, who landed in a deplorable state, unfit for service, a great many men having died soon after. They were suffering from malignant fever.[7] All the sick, officers and privates, were conveyed to our hospital, which was insufficient to contain them; we were therefore compelled to fill most parts of the building, even to the church, having obtained the permission of the late bishop Pontbriand, our illustrious prelate. His great zeal and charity, all must readily acknowledge, being desirous of partaking in the labors of the Almoners, passing days and nights in ministering to the sick and

5 The *Hôtel Dieu* (nunnery) had been recently destroyed by fire, communicated by an incendiary [note added in the original edition].

6 Or Governor [note added in the original edition].

7 *Malignant fever*: typhus.

dying;[8] exposing his life in the midst of infection, which contributed materially to affect his health and to abridge his days. He had the misfortune to lose four of his Almoners, who perished in a few days from the pestilential infection they inhaled in their attendance upon the sick.[9] He ministered to them himself, and his charitable attentions were readily bestowed upon his flock generally. The heavy duties with which we were charged, seemed to touch his noble heart; the loss of ten of our youngest nuns affected him most sensibly. In their last moments they were not without consolation, conscious of having done their duty. They prayed that God would be pleased to receive them as acceptable victims in appeasing his wroth; but this was only a small portion of the bitter cup of affliction prepared for us. The loss deprived us of the power to attend to all the calls upon us, arising from our numerous patients. The bishop caused ten nuns to come to our assistance from the *Hôtel Dieu* of Québec; who, full of a sense of their duty, really edified us by their exertions, and indefatigable zeal, in attending day and night upon the sick. Our gratitude toward their community increased from day to day. The poverty of our establishment did not admit of our assisting them in their distress as we desired, their house having been destroyed by fire.

Let us now, dear Mothers, endeavor to give you some details of a war and captivity, which our sins have drawn upon us. Heaven, so far favorable to our supplications, preserved us on several occasions. The most holy Virgin, patroness of this country, having baffled the efforts of the enemy enabled our vessels to escape their vigilance, and the tempests and storms of the ocean. But alas! want of sufficient gratitude, deprived us of a continuation of her protection. Still, during the first attacks of our enemy, we continued to enjoy it; everywhere they appeared, they were beaten and repulsed with considerable loss. The taking of_____,[10] of Fort St George and several others, of which they were deprived, are proofs. The victories we obtained at *Belle Rivière* and at *Carillon*,[11] were most glorious; our warriors returned crowned with laurels. They probably did not return thanks to the God of armies, to whom they were indebted for success, as it was miraculous; their small numbers, without heavenly aid, could not so completely have accomplished it. Thereupon, the enemy, despairing of vanquishing us, ashamed to retreat, determined to fit out a formidable fleet, armed with all the artillery that the infernal regions could supply for the destruction of humankind. They displayed the British flag in the harbor of Québec on the 26th June, 1759. On the receipt of intelligence

8 *Almoner*: military chaplains, serving as assistants to the priest who holds the official title.

9 *Pestilential infection*: any of several overwhelming and often deadly diseases. Following an episode of the plague in Marseilles in 1720, Dr Richard Mead (1673–1754) released a pamphlet on the spreading of diseases, including pestilential infections, based on which the British government first formulated a quarantine response. The theories espoused in the document would be debated for decades. This would seem to indicate that the Augustinian Nuns in Québec supported and adopted his theories.

10 Fort Chouaguin probably [note added in the original edition].

11 *Belle Rivière*: see footnote 8, p.96.

of their arrival, our troops and militia came down from above. Our generals left garrisons in the advanced posts, of which there is a great number above Montréal, in order to prevent the junction of their land forces, which it was understood were on the march. Our generals did not fail to occupy most points where the enemy might land; but they could not guard them all. The sickness suffered by our troops, lately from France, and the losses they sustained in two or three recent actions with the enemy, though victorious, weakened us considerably; and it became necessary to abandon Pointe de Lévy directly opposite to and commanding Québec. The enemy soon occupied it and constructed their batteries; which commenced firing on the 24th July, in a manner to excite the greatest alarm in our unfortunate communities of religious ladies.

The Reverend Mother St Helen, Superior of the Hospital,[12] wrote to us the same day, supplicating admission into our house, for herself and her Sisters. Although we could not doubt that our building would be speedily filled with wounded from the siege, we received our dear Sisters with open arms. The tears which we shed and the tenderness exhibited toward them made it evident that we were happy to share with them the little comfort that remained to us. We surrendered the rooms to them, and confined ourselves to our dormitories. We were not long before another dislodgement took place. Next day at six o'clock in the evening, we beheld in our windows the Reverend Ladies of the Ursuline Convent,[13] who seized with fright, occasioned by the shot and shells, which had penetrated the walls of their dwelling, were hurrying toward our asylum. It became necessary to find place for upward of thirty Sisters, who were received with no less tenderness and affection than was exhibited to the ladies of the hospital.

It now became necessary to ascertain how we should accommodate ourselves. On the arrival of the English fleet, all the families of distinction, merchants, &c. capable of maintaining themselves, were removed to Trois Rivières and Montréal, thereby relieving the garrison during the siege. Several members of our families and others whom we could not refuse, sought shelter with us, being at hand to succor their husbands and sons who were wounded. As our house was beyond the range of the enemy's artillery, the poor people of the city did not fail to seek refuge there. All the out-houses, stables, barns, garrets &c. were well filled.

The only consolation we enjoyed was that of daily seeing our Bishop, tho' in a dying state, exhorting and encouraging us not to relax in our good works. He was induced to retire from his capital, his palace and cathedral being reduced to

12 *Hôtel Dieu*, the first Augustinian hospital in Québec, located in the NE part of the city, within the Côte du Palais and the Rue des Ramparts in the upper town, well within range of the British guns.

13 The Ursuline church and convent were located nearly at the center of the upper town. Arriving in Canada in 1639, the Sisters learned the languages of the natives and began their service as teachers, especially for young girls and women. After his death, the Marquis de Montcalm was buried in a bomb crater within the monastery chapel, until 2001 when his remains were moved to a mausoleum in the General Hospital Cemetery, where he now rests with hundreds of his men.

ashes. He would not quit his flock while any hope remained of saving them; he lived with the curate of Charlesbourgh, three miles from Québec. He permitted the several Almoners to celebrate Mass in our Choir, the church being occupied by the wounded. Most people of the neighborhood assisted at Mass, so that we were extremely crowded. It was consolatory to us, that we were enabled to have divine service during the siege, without interfering with the attentions to the sick and wounded. The only rest we partook of, was during prayers, and still it was not without interruption from the noise of shells and shot, dreading every moment that they would be directed toward us. The red-hot shot and *carcasses* terrified those who attended the sick during the night. They had the affliction of witnessing the destruction of the houses of the citizens, many of our connections being immediately interested therein. During one night, upward of fifty of the best houses in the lower town were destroyed. The vaults containing merchandise and many precious articles, did not escape the effects of the artillery. During this dreadful conflagration, we could offer nothing but our tears and prayers at the foot of the altar at such moments as could be snatched from the necessary attention to the wounded.

In addition to these misfortunes, we had to contend with more than one enemy; famine, at all times inseparable from war, threatened to reduce us to the last extremity;[14] upward of six hundred persons in our building and vicinity, partaking of our small means of subsistence, supplied from the government stores; which were likely soon to be short of what was required for the troops. In the midst of this desolation, the Almighty, disposed to humble us, and to deprive us of our substance, which we had probably amassed contrary to his will, and with too great avidity, still mercifully preserved our lives, which were daily periled, from the present state of the country.

Our enemy, informed of our destitute condition, was satisfied with battering our walls, despairing of vanquishing us, except by starvation. The river was the only obstruction we could oppose to the enemy; it likewise interfered to prevent our attacking them. They remained long under our eyes, meditating a descent; finally they determined upon landing at Beauport. Our army, always on the alert, being apprised by the advanced guard, immediately rushed to the spot, with that ardor natural to the French nation, without calculating upon the many causes likely to wrest the victory from their grasp.

The enemy, more cautious in their proceedings, on observing our army, hesitated in landing all their forces. We drove them from our redoubts, of which they had obtained possession. They became overwhelmed, and left the field strewed

14 It was not war alone which rendered New France on the brink of starvation. Poor harvests in 1756 and 1757 greatly reduced the available supplies, as well as the expulsion of the Acadians from their farms in the *maritimes*, who had been providing crops and cattle for the strained interior settlements. By the time the Royal Navy cut off all supply from France, the residents were already in significant peril.

with killed and wounded. This action alone, had it been properly managed, would have finally relieved us from their invasion. We must not, however, attribute the mismanagement solely to our generals; the Indian tribes, often essential to our support, became prejudicial to us on this occasion. Their hideous yells of defiance tended to intimidate our foes, who instead of meeting the onset, to which they had exposed themselves, precipitately retreated to their boats, and left us masters of the field. We charitably conveyed their wounded to our hospital, notwithstanding the fury and rage of the Indians, who, according their cruel custom, sought to scalp them. Our army continued constantly ready to oppose the enemy. They dared not attempt a second landing; but ashamed of inaction, they took to burning the country places. Under shelter of darkness, they moved their vessels about seven or eight leagues above Québec. There they captured a great number of prisoners, including women and children, who had taken refuge in that quarter. There again they experienced the valor of a small garrison of invalids, commanded by an officer, having one arm only, placed there in charge of military stores. The enemy, after a severe struggle, succeeded in capturing them.[15]

After remaining in vain nearly three months at anchor in the port, they appeared disposed to retire, despairing of success; but the Almighty, whose intentions are beyond our penetration, and always just, having resolved to subdue us, inspired the English commander with the idea of making another attempt before his departure, which was done by surprise during the night. It was the intention, that night, to send supplies to a body of troops forming an outpost on the heights near Québec. A miserable deserter gave the information to the enemy, and persuaded them that it would be easy to surprise us, and pass their boats by using our countersign. They profited by the information, and the treasonable scheme succeeded. They landed on giving the password; the officer detected the deceit, but too late. He defended his post bravely with his small band, and was wounded. By this plan the enemy found themselves on the heights near the city. *Général* de Montcalm, without loss of time, marched at the head of his army; but having to proceed about half a league, the enemy, had time to bring up their artillery, and to form for the reception of the French. Our leading battalions did not wait the arrival and formation of the other forces to support them, they rushed with their usual impetuosity on their enemies and killed a great number; but they were soon overcome by the artillery. They lost their general and a great number of officers. Our loss was not equal to that of the enemy; but it was not the less serious. *Général* de Montcalm and his principal officers fell on the occasion.[16]

15 Most likely a reference to the 20 August British landing at Deschambault, though I have found no other reference to Paul Perrault (see footnote 109, p.53) as having only one arm. And while property was destroyed in the attack, the post was not captured. The British were driven off by the arrival of French cavalry under M. de la Roche-Beaucourt followed by M. de Bougainville with grenadiers.

16 It is the memorable battle of the 13th September, 1759, which took place on the Plains of Abraham, that is alluded to. The official account of the English loss on this occasion is as follows:

Several officers of the Canadian militia, fathers of families, shared the same fate. We witnessed the carnage from our windows. It was in such a scene that charity triumphed, and caused us to forget self-preservation and the danger we were exposed to, in the immediate presence of the enemy. We were in the midst of the dead and the dying, who were brought in to us by hundreds, many of them our close connections; it was necessary to smother our griefs and exert ourselves to relieve them. Loaded with the inmates of three convents, and all the inhabitants of the neighboring suburbs, which the approach of the enemy caused to fly in this direction, you may judge of our terror and confusion.[17] The enemy masters of the field, and within a few paces of our house. Exposed to the fury of the soldiers, we had reason to dread the worst. It was then that we experienced the truth of the words of holy writ: 'He who places his trust in the Lord has nothing to fear.'

But tho' not wanting in faith or hope, the approach of night greatly added to our fears. The three Sisterhoods, with the exception of those who were dispersed over the house, prostrated themselves the foot of the altar, to implore divine mercy. The silence and consternation which prevailed, was suddenly interrupted by loud and repeated knocks at our doors. Two young nuns, who were carrying broth to the sick, unavoidably happened to be near when the door was opened. The pallor and fright which overcame them, touched the officer, and he prevented the guard from entering; he demanded the appearance of the Superiors, and desired then to assure us of protection; he said that part of the English force would enter and take possession of the house, apprehending that our army, which was not distant, might return and attack them, in their entrenchments; – which would certainly have taken place had our troops been enabled to reassemble before the capitulation. Soon after we saw their army drawn up under our windows. The loss we had sustained the day before led us to fear, with reason, that our fate was decided, our people being unable to rally. *Général* de Lévis, second in command, who became chief on the death of de Montcalm, had set out, some days previous, with about 3,000 men, to reinforce the upper posts, which were daily harassed by the enemy.

The loss we had just sustained, and the departure of that force, determined the Marquis de Vaudreuil, Governor-General of the Colony, to abandon Québec, being

Officers, serjeants, and privates killed	61
Officers, serjeants, drummers, and privates wounded	598
Soldiers missing	5
Total	664

After the battle, several French officers admitted their loss amounted to nearly 1,500 men, killed, wounded and prisoners. [note added in the original edition].

17 The General Hospital had received a communication from Wolfe, as a part of his recognition for the French rescue and care for Captain David Ochterlony (see footnote 90, p.46), assuring them that, should the British prevail, the hospital would be under his personal protection and not harmed in any way. Word of this promise had spread into the community and they had swarmed the hospital seeking its safety for themselves. A promise Soeur de la Visitation chose to omit in the telling of her tale.

no longer able to retain it. The enemy having formed their entrenchments and their Camp, near the principal gate; their fleet commanding the port, it was impossible to convey succor to the garrison. Mr de Ramezay, who commanded, with a feeble garrison, without provisions or munitions, held out to the last extremity.

The principal inhabitants represented to him that they had readily sacrificed their property, but with regard to their wives and children, they could not make up their minds to witness their massacre, in the event of the place being stormed; it was therefore necessary to determine on capitulation.

The English readily accorded the articles demanded, religious toleration and civil advantages for the inhabitants. Happy in having acquired possession of a country, in which they had on several previous occasions failed, they were the most moderate of conquerors. We could not, without injustice, complain of the manner in which they treated us. However, their good treatment has not yet dried our tears. We do not shed them as did the good Hebrews near the waters of Babylon, we are still in the land of promise; but our canticles will not again be heard until we can shake off this medley of nations, and until our temples are re-established; then we will celebrate, with the utmost gratitude, the merciful bounty of the Lord.

After the capitulation of Québec, all that remained of the families of distinction followed the French army to Montréal. His lordship the Bishop, having no place to dwell in, was compelled to follow their example. Before his departure, he made all necessary arrangements in his diocese; he appointed Mr Briand Vicar General, who is justly considered a godly man, and of such established merit, that our enemies could not with-hold their approbation, and, I may say, their veneration of him.[18] He maintained his rights and those of his curates, in such a manner as to meet with no obstacles from the English. The Vicar selected our house for his residence; beholding us charged with an infinite number of people, without resources, exposed to many evils, – he did not consider us safe but under his own eyes. He was not mistaken; and, in the end, we were much indebted to him.

The reduction of Québec, on the 18th September, 1759, produced no tranquility for us, but rather increased our labors. The English generals came to our hospital

18 Jean-Olivier Briand (1715–1794), Bishop of Québec, studied at the *Séminaire* de Saint-Brieuc and was ordained a priest in March 1739, in 1741 became a missionary in Canada. As the time of the siege approached he found himself serving as canon, treasurer of the chapter, confessor of the Augustinian nuns of the *Hôtel Dieu* and the *Hôpital Général*, supervising a group of young seminarians, as well as secretary of the bishop. Appointed Vicar General on 13 September 1759. When Bishop Pontbriand died in June of 1760 it threw the leadership of the church in Canada into turmoil. All communication with France was cut off and no new bishop could be sent. In such a case it was up to the chapter to select a new leader – though the travel restrictions imposed by the British prevented their meeting until July. The chapter named three Vicars General for Canada, one of whom was Briand. The chapter at that time also identified him as 'at the head and the first of the vicars general, the see being vacant.' Briand was bishop in all but title. After years of trials and challenges he was consecrated Bishop on 16 March 1766. André Vachon, 'Briand, Jean-Olivier', in *Dictionary of Canadian Biography*, vol.4 (Toronto: University of Toronto/Université Laval, 2003–).

and assured us of their protection, and at the same time, required us to take charge of their wounded and sick.

Although we were near the seat of war, our establishment had nothing to fear, as the well-understood rights of nations protected hospitals so situated, still they obliged us to lodge a guard of thirty men, and it was necessary to prepare food and bedding for them. On being relieved they carried off many of the blankets, &c. the officer taking no measures to prevent them. Our greatest misfortune was to hear their talking during divine service.

The Sisters from the other convents determined to return to their former dwellings. It was very painful for us to part with them. Their long residence with us, and the esteem and affection created thereby caused our separation to be most sensibly felt. The Reverend Mother St Helen, Superior, observing us overwhelmed with work, which was daily augmenting, left us twelve of her dear Sisters, who were a great relief to us. Two of the Ursuline Sisters were too weak to be removed, and they terminated their days with us. The fatigues and sickness they endured, with much patience and resignation, merited I trust, an eternal reward. The departure of the dear Sisters, gave us no additional space, as it became necessary to place the sick of the English army in the same apartments.

Let us now return to the French. Our generals not finding their force sufficient to undertake the recovery of their losses, proceeded to the construction of a fort, about five leagues above Québec, and left a garrison therein, capable of checking the enemy from penetrating into the country.[19] They did not remain inactive, but were constantly on the alert, harassing the enemy. The English were not safe beyond the gates of Québec. General Murray the commander of the place, on several occasions was near being made a prisoner; and would not have escaped if our people had been faithful. Prisoners were frequently made, which so irritated the commander, that he sent out detachments to pillage and burn the habitations of the country people.

The desire to recover the country and to acquire glory, was attended with great loss to our citizens. We heard of nothing but combats throughout the winter; the severity of the season had not the effect of making them lay down their arms.

19 Immediately following the surrender of Québec, the two armies were forced to prepare for the severe Canadian winter. Monckton returned to New York, Townshend headed for England, and Brigadier Murray was left as governor in Québec. Saunders released all but a few small ships to sail for winter port in Halifax, with orders to return when the ice cleared in the spring. In Québec City what food was available was of questionable quality. Most of the garrison would be suffering from scurvy by spring. With the vast destruction of the buildings within the city, adequate housing was in short supply. Murray passed the winter and spring strengthening his defenses, repairing entrenchments, building blockhouses, establishing defended posts at Cap Rouge, Sillery, Pointe de Lévy, and at St Foi, as well a repairing and reinforcing the redoubt and church there. Perhaps it is one of these works to which she refers. Government of Canada, 'The Battle of Sainte-Foy', *National Battlefields Commission: Plains of Abraham*, http://bataille.ccbn-nbc.gc.ca/en/bataille-de-sainte-foy/contexte/un-hiver-difficile-a-quebec.php (accessed 29 August 2018).

Wherever the enemy was observed, they were pursued without relaxation; which caused them to remark, 'that they had never known a people more attached and faithful to their sovereign than the Canadians.'

The English did not fail to require the oath of allegiance to their King; but, notwithstanding this forced obligation, which our people did not consider themselves bound to observe, they joined the flying camps of the French, whenever an opportunity offered.

The French forces did not spare the inhabitants of the country; they lived freely at the expense of those unfortunate people. We suffered considerable loss in a *seigneurie* which we possessed below Québec.[20] The officer commanding seized on all our cattle, which were numerous, and wheat to subsist his troops. The purveyor rendered us no account of such seizures. Notwithstanding this loss, we were compelled to maintain upward of three hundred wounded, sent to us after the battle of the 13th September.

The stores of the French government, now in the possession of the English, being exhausted, we were therefore obliged to have recourse to the enemy. They gave us flour and clothing. But how little suited was it for our unfortunate wounded! We had no wine nor other comforts to afford them, Drained long since by the great numbers, nothing remained but goodwill. This however did not satisfy them. Our officers represented to the English commander that they were not accustomed to be treated in that manner by the King of France. The commander, piqued by this reproach, attached the blame to us, and required us to make a statement of what was necessary for the relief of these gentlemen, and then caused us to pay for it. We flattered ourselves that the French government, more just, would be proud to reimburse all our extra expenses, which were unavoidable at this time. The desire to obtain our rights and recover the country, induced us to do our utmost in support of the cause.

As we had in our hospital many French soldiers of the garrison of Québec, and of the sufferers in the action of the 13th, they implored us, when their strength was re-established, to allow them to fly and join the army; we readily agreed to it, and furnished them with clothing and provisions, to enable them to accomplish their object, which drew upon us the most severe reproaches and menaces from the enemy. They threatened to allow us to die from starvation.

As our house was still full of sick, the Grand Vicar, who attended closely to our welfare, removed several of the Almoners, who contributed to embarrass us, from the scarcity of provisions. He and the Reverend Mr de Rigauville, our chaplain, administered to the sick, and attended them in their last moments, night and day.[21]

20 The *seigneurie* de Saint-Vallier, in the Chaudière-Appalaches region, overlooks the Rivière St Laurent, Isle d'Orléans, and Québec City. Part of this *seigneurie* was purchased in 1720 by Monsignor Jean-Baptiste de La Croix de Chevrières de Saint-Vallier, founder of the General Hospital. The convent and hospital would later sell the property toward meeting their debts incurred during the siege.

21 Charles-Régis Blaise Des Bergères de Rigauville (1724–1780) Native of Québec City, son of a military officer and landholder, entered the Jesuit College in Québec at the age of 16. He was ordained a Catholic

We have at this time upward of two hundred English, who occupy our dining rooms and dormitories; and as many French, in our infirmaries, leaving us merely one small room to retire into. There assembled, and left to our reflections, we anticipated the worst. All communication with our friends being interrupted, we knew not what was passing in the upper parts. Our enemies, better informed, announced the approach of our army; the measures they adopted, and the additional fortifications they constructed in Québec, supported by a strong garrison, caused us to dread the result of the struggle. On our side we had false prophets; women painting in their imaginations sieges, without mortars or cannon; the town taken by assault. Nothing more was required to stir and animate those who were eager for the fray.

As soon as the season appeared suitable for campaigning, our army followed the ice, scantily provided with provisions, and still less with artillery suited for a siege. Our generals did not doubt the valor of the troops; but they only flattered themselves with the prospect of success, in the event of the arrival of succor from France. In the expectation of their arrival, our army commenced their march; they arrived near Québec on the 26th April. The 27th was employed in landing the few guns brought from Montréal. An artilleryman in landing, fell on a loose piece of ice, which floated him directly opposite to the city. The extraordinary conveyance attracted the attention of the sentinels; they notified the commander, who immediately sent relief to the artilleryman. He was brought before the commander, and questioned. The poor man, seized with fright, after his dangerous escape, was quite unprepared for evasion; he candidly acknowledged that he was one of the French army, who were within two leagues of Québec. He related how he had been transported down the river against his will. So far the march of the army had been secret. The secret being now developed, it appeared to us a bad omen; an event governed by a power beyond our reach or opposition. The English commander, General Murray, informed by this means, lost not a moment. He immediately withdrew a strong advanced post, stationed about a league from Québec, with their cannon, and blew up the church of St Foi, which had served as a shelter for the troops; after which he summoned a council of war, and appeared to be alone of opinion that it was expedient to march out with a considerable portion of the garrison, and take up a strong position, establish his batteries, and there meet the enemy. This proposal did not meet with the sanction of the majority; but, notwithstanding, he carried it into execution.

priest on 20 September 1749. In 1752 he was named Canon of the cathedral in Québec, remaining in that position until his death. Also named chaplain of the General Hospital in 1759 and Superior of the Community in 1768. In 1739, at his father's passing, he became the *Sieur* of Berthier-en-Bas, an estate he bequeathed to Québec General Hospital. Government of Québec, 'Blaise of the Bergeres de Rigauville, Charles-Régis', *Directory of Québec's Cultural Heritage*, http://www.patrimoine-culturel.gouv.qc.ca/rpcq/detail.do?methode=consulter&id=18462&type=pge#.XBQTH2j0m00 (accessed 13 June 2019).

Our army, ignorant of the information accidentally obtained by the garrison, continued their march. During the night of the 27th and 28th it rained incessantly. The heavens appeared to contend against us. The thunder and lightning, very rare at this season, seemed to be the forerunner of the shock to which our forces were about to be exposed. The rain falling in torrents, and the roads rendered impracticable by the melting of the snow, prevented their [the army's] marching in good order. General de Bourlamaque,[22] second in command, at the head of the leading battalions, came in sight of the enemy before forming his men. The enemy's artillery lost no time in opening a destructive fire upon them, which placed many *hors de combat.*[23] The general was wounded and forced to retire. The main body of our troops, marines and militia, better acquainted with the roads, arrived in time to support a regiment, which was near being cut to pieces, rather than retreat. The action then became most furious and general. The English having had the choice of position, possessed considerable advantage. Our army did not expect to find their foes drawn up in order of battle; they were consequently compelled to halt, and not finding the ground suitable for extending their lines, the first divisions had to bear the brunt of the fire. The main struggle took place near Québec, on a height opposite our house. Not a shot was fired which did not resound in our ears. Judge, if possible, what must have been our situation; the interest of our country, and our close connections were amongst the combatants, producing a state of anguish it is impossible to paint. The Grand Vicar, at present our Bishop, who suffered equally with us, exhorted us to bear the shock with resignation and submission to the decrees of the Almighty; after which he retired to the church, penetrated with the deepest affliction, and threw himself at the foot of the altar, where he poured forth his prayers, imploring with confidence that the divine ruler of events would be pleased to stay the deadly conflict, and spare the flock confided to his care. He then arose full of hope, in order to proceed to the field of battle, notwithstanding our remonstrances, which were not urged without reason, as he must be exposed to great danger. He was induced to proceed to the field, because he apprehended that there were not a sufficient number of clergy on the spot to minister to the dying, who he believed were very numerous.

Mr de Rigauville, our chaplain, full of zeal, was desirous of following the Grand Vicar. He was not without anxiety, his only brother, and several of his nearest connections being in the army. He had the satisfaction of seeing the enemy turn their backs and fly. The engagement lasted two hours. The intrepidity and valor of the French and Canadians drove the enemy from their strong position, and followed them up under the guns of the city. We remained masters of the field, and of their cannon, and made many prisoners. The enemy retired within the walls,

22 *François-Charles de Bourlamaque*: see footnote 82, p.38.

23 *Hors de combat*: out of action.

and dared not again venture out. The victory, however, was dearly bought, and caused many tears to flow.[24]

M. de Lévis, on approaching Québec, assembled a council; it was proposed to blow up our house, fearing that it might be a rallying point for the enemy. But God was pleased to spare us and them; he opened their eyes, and convinced them that it was most essential to their purposes. The French commander directed us to dismiss all persons who had taken refuge in our establishment, as he looked to us as the only persons capable of taking charge of the wounded during the siege, about to be commenced. We did not fail to answer, that we would proceed to empty our house, with the exception of two hundred English sick, which it was not in our power to remove; but in other respects we were always ready to second his intentions, and to render all the service in our power.

After the battle he [the French commander] sent us an officer with a French guard, which however, did not free us from the English guard. It became necessary to find room for them. But this was but the prelude to what was yet to happen. It would require another pen than mine to depict the horrors which we were compelled to witness, during twenty-four hours, which were occupied in the reception of the wounded; their cries and the lamentations of their friends were truly heart-rending. It required supernatural strength to bear such scenes.

After having prepared upward of five hundred beds, which were procured from the public stores, as many more were required. Our stables and barns, were filled with these unfortunate men: it was very difficult to find time to attend to all. We had in our infirmaries seventy-two officers, thirty-three of whom died. We saw nothing but amputation of legs and arms. To crown our distress there was a deficiency of linen; we were under the necessity of giving our sheets and our body-linen. The French army did not fail to provide that article, but unfortunately, the vessel conveying their stores from Montréal was captured by the English.

In this instance we were differently situated from what we were after the battle of the 13th September; we could not expect assistance from the religious ladies of the city; the English had taken possession of their establishments for the reception of their wounded, who were more numerous than the French. About twenty officers of the English army, who were left wounded on the field, were also brought to us.

Reverend Mothers, as I give you this account, merely from memory, of what passed under our eyes, and with a view to afford you the satisfaction of knowing that we sustained with fortitude and in an edifying manner the painful duties, imposed upon us by our vocation; I will not undertake to relate to you all the particulars of the surrender of the country. I could do it but imperfectly, and from hearsay. I will merely say that the majority of the Canadians were disposed to perish rather than surrender; and that the small number of troops remaining were

24 This engagement is commonly called the Battle of St Foi, 28 April 1760, with over 800 French casualties and over 1,000 British.

deficient of ammunition and provisions, and only surrendered in order to save the lives of the women and children, who are likely to be exposed to the greatest peril where towns are carried by assault.

Alas! dear Mothers, it was a great misfortune for us that France could not send, in the spring, some vessels with provisions and munitions; we should still be under her dominion. She has lost a vast country and a faithful people, sincerely attached to their sovereign; a loss we must greatly deplore, on account of our religion, and the difference of the laws to which we must submit. We vainly flatter ourselves that peace may restore us to our rights; and that the Almighty will treat us in a fatherly manner, and soon cease to humble us; we still continue to experience his wrath. Our sins, doubtless, are very great, which leads us to apprehend that we are doomed to suffer long; the spirit of repentance is not general with the people, and God is still offended. We, however, yet entertain the hope of again coming under the dominion of our former masters.

You must, no doubt, have learnt that the English, moved by our importunities, have granted us a Bishop for this unfortunate colony. The choice of both governments has fallen upon the Reverend Jean Olivier Briand.[25] It is unnecessary that I should dwell upon his merits; they are well-known. Without his protection and intercession our convent and property would have been sold to satisfy the debts, contracted to support the French troops; our creditors were compelled by order of the English governor, to desist from their prosecutions. To him our establishment is indebted for its present existence. The French government is indebted to us in the sum of one hundred and twenty thousand *livres*, for expenses incurred in the maintenance of French troops. We look for no compensation for our services, He to whom we devote ourselves will recompense us amply. It is said that we will have to depend upon the public for support: we cannot believe it, as the English government, having witnessed the expenses we have incurred, will plead our cause with France, and not allow us to suffer such serious loss.

[The memoire ends, unsigned.]

25 His appointment has been simplified here. On 15 September 1763, Vicar General Étienne Montgolfier was chosen by the chapter to be the new Bishop of Québec. General Murray stymied this appointment, preferring Briand, who had already proven himself adept at working successfully with the British administration. Montgolfier withdrew from consideration in September of 1764. On 11 September, the chapter gathered at the General Hospital and unanimously elected Briand to be put forward for the position. Briand sailed for England, to present himself, but no one in Great Britain knew exactly how to make him a bishop. It was determined that he need only present himself in France and be consecrated there, if he was willing to function under the title of Superintendent of the Catholic church in Canada. He went to France and was quietly consecrated in Paris on 16 March 1766. Vachon, 'Briand, Jean-Olivier'.

Bibliography

Printed Sources

Anon., *Journal du Siège de Québec du 10 Mai au 18 Septembre 1759* (ed. Aegidius Fauteux) (Québec: Bibliothécaire de Saint-Sulpice, 1922).

Blais, Marie-Céline, 'Tarieu de La Naudière, Charles-François,' in *Dictionary of Canadian Biography*, vol.4 (Toronto: University of Toronto/Université Laval, 2003–).

Brisson, Réal, 'Juchereau Duchesnay, Antoine,' in *Dictionary of Canadian Biography*, vol.5 (Toronto: University of Toronto/Université Laval, 2003–).

Castonguay, Jacques, 'Aubert de Gaspé, Ignace-Philippe', in *Dictionary of Canadian Biography*, vol.4 (Toronto: University of Toronto/Université Laval, 2003–).

Corley, Nora T., 'Legardeur de Courtemanche, Augustin', in *Dictionary of Canadian Biography*, vol.2 (Toronto: University of Toronto/Université Laval, 2003–).

Doughty, Arthur, and Parmelee, George W. (eds.), *The Siege of Quebec and the Battle of the Plains of Abraham* (6 vols), vol.6 (Québec: Dessault & Proulx, 1901).

Douglas, W.A.B., 'Durell, Philip,' in *Dictionary of Canadian Biography*, vol.3 (Toronto: University of Toronto/Université Laval, 2003–).

Dubé, Paul-André, 'Legardeur de Repentigny, Pierre (1657–1736)', in *Dictionary of Canadian Biography*, vol.2 (Toronto: University of Toronto/Université Laval, 2003–).

Dufour, Pierre, 'Boucher de Niverville, Joseph', in *Dictionary of Canadian Biography*, vol.5 (Toronto: University of Toronto/Université Laval, 2003–).

Eccles, W.J., 'Lévis, François de, Duc de Lévis,' in Dictionary of Canadian Biography, vol.4 (Toronto: University of Toronto/Université Laval, 2003–).

Eccles, W.J., 'Montcalm, Louis-Joseph, Marquis de Montcalm,' in *Dictionary of Canadian Biography*, vol.3 (Toronto: University of Toronto/Université Laval, 2003–).

Eccles, W.J., 'Rigaud de Vaudreuil de Cavagnial, Pierre de, Marquis de Vaudreuil', in *Dictionary of Canadian Biography*, vol.4 (Toronto: University of Toronto/Université Laval, 2003-).

Eccles, W.J., 'Senezergues de la Rodde, Étienne-Guillaume de,' in *Dictionary of Canadian Biography*, vol.3 (Toronto: University of Toronto/Université Laval, 2003–).

Foligné, François Jérôme, *Journal des Faits Arrivés à l'Armé de Québec, Capital dans l'Amérique Septentrional, Pendant la Campagne de l'Année 1759, par M. de Foligné* (Québec: The Community of Franciscan Sisters, 1901).

Frenière, André, 'Panet, Jean-Claude,' in *Dictionary of Canadian Biography*, vol.4 (Toronto: University of Toronto/Université Laval, 2003–).

Gallup, Andrew and Donald F. Schaffer, *La Marine: The French Colonial Soldier in Canada 1745–1761* (Bowie, MD: Heritage Books, 1992).

Igartua, José, 'Amiot, Jean-Baptiste (1717–69)', in *Dictionary of Canadian Biography*, vol.3 (Toronto: University of Toronto/Université Laval, 2003–).

Lachance, André, 'Grasset de Saint-Sauveur, André', *Dictionary of Canadian Biography*, vol.4 (Toronto: University of Toronto/ Université Laval, 2003–).

Lachance, André, 'Poulin de Courval, François-Louis,' in *Dictionary of Canadian Biography*, vol.3 (Toronto: University of Toronto/Université Laval, 2003–).

Laramie, Michael G., 'The French Lake Champlain fleet and the contest for the control of the lake, 1742–1760', *Vermont History*, 80:1 (2012), pp.1–32.

Phyllis E. Leblanc, 'Deschamps de Boishébert et de Raffetot, Charles', in *Dictionary of Canadian Biography*, vol.4 (Toronto: University of Toronto/Université Laval, 2003–).

Lemoine, Sir James MacPherson (ed.), *Manuscripts Relating to the Early History of Canada*, 4th Series (Québec: Dawson & Co., 1875).

Lemoine, Sir James MacPherson, *Quebec, Past and Present: A History of Quebec, 1608–1876*, vol.2 (Québec: Augustin Coté & Co., 1876).

MacLeod, Malcolm, 'Perrault, Paul,' in *Dictionary of Canadian Biography*, vol.3 (Toronto: University of Toronto/Université Laval, 2003–).

Mathieu, Jacques, 'Daine, François', in *Dictionary of Canadian Biography*, vol.3 (Toronto: University of Toronto/Université Laval, 2003–).

Miquelon, Dale, 'Lefebvre, Jean', in *Dictionary of Canadian Biography*, vol.3 (Toronto: University of Toronto/Université Laval, 2003–).

Moogk, Peter N., 'Pouchot, Pierre', in *Dictionary of Canadian Biography*, vol.3 (Toronto: University of Toronto/Université Laval, 2003–).

Pariseau, Jean, 'Le Mercier, François-Marc-Antoine,' in *Dictionary of Canadian Biography*, vol.4 (Toronto: University of Toronto/Université Laval, 2003–).

Pothier, Bernard, 'Dupont de Chambon de Vergor, Louis', in *Dictionary of Canadian Biography*, vol.4 (Toronto: University of Toronto/Université Laval, 2003–).

Pritchard, James S., 'Kanon, Jacques,' in *Dictionary of Canadian Biography*, vol.3 (Toronto: University of Toronto/Université Laval, 2003–).

Pritchard, James S., 'Pellegrin, Gabriel', in *Dictionary of Canadian Biography*, vol.4 (Toronto: University of Toronto/Université Laval, 2003–).

Raffle, William (ed.), *Glories to Useless Heroism: The American Journals of Comte Maurès de Malartic, 1755–1760* (Solihull: Helion & Company, 2017).

Rousseau, François, 'Vienne, François-Joseph de,' in *Dictionary of Canadian Biography*, vol.4 (Toronto: University of Toronto/Université Laval, 2003–).

Roy, Julie, 'Marie-Joseph Legardeur de Repentigny, *Mère Supérieure Hospitalière* (Canada, 1693–Canada, 1776)', in Gaston Deschênes and Denis Vaugeois (eds.), *Vivre la Conquête*, vol.2 (Lille: Septentrion, 2014), pp.148–157.

Russ, C.J., 'Hertel de Saint-François, Étienne,' in *Dictionary of Canadian Biography*, vol.3 (Toronto: University of Toronto/Université Laval, 2003–).

Russ, C.J., 'La Corne, Louis de, Chevalier de La Corne', in *Dictionary of Canadian Biography*, vol.3 (Toronto: University of Toronto/Université Laval, 2003–).

Russ, C.J., 'Le Marchand de Lignery, François-Marie,' in *Dictionary of Canadian Biography*, vol.3 (Toronto: University of Toronto/Université Laval, 2003–).

Saint-Père, Rameau de, *Une Colonie Féodale en Amérique L'Acadie (1604–1881)*, vol.2 (Montréal: Granger Frères, 1889).

Stacey, C.P., 'Bourlamaque, François-Charles de', in *Dictionary of Canadian Biography*, vol.3 (Toronto: University of Toronto/Université Laval, 2003–).

Stacey, C.P., 'Wolfe, James', in *Dictionary of Canadian Biography*, vol.3 (Toronto: University of Toronto/Université Laval, 2003–).

Taillemite, Étienne, 'Bougainville, Louis-Antoine de, Comte de Bougainville,' in *Dictionary of Canadian Biography*, vol.5 (Toronto: University of Toronto/Université Laval, 2003–).

Taillemite, Étienne, 'Dumas, Jean-Daniel', in *Dictionary of Canadian Biography*, vol.4 (Toronto: University of Toronto/Université Laval, 2003–).

Taillemite, Étienne, 'Legardeur de Repentigny, Louis,' in *Dictionary of Canadian Biography*, vol.4 (Toronto: University of Toronto/Université Laval, 2003–).

Thorpe, F.J., 'Chaussegros de Léry, Gaspard-Joseph (1721–97)', in *Dictionary of Canadian Biography*, vol.4 (Toronto: University of Toronto/Université Laval, 2003–).

Thorpe, F.J., 'Sarrebource de Pontleroy, Nicolas,' in *Dictionary of Canadian Biography*, vol.5 (Toronto: University of Toronto/Université Laval, 2003–).

Thwaites, Reuben Gold (ed.), 'The French regime in Wisconsin – II 1727–1748', in *Collections of the State Historical Society of Wisconsin*, vol.17 (Madison, WI: published by the Society, 1906).

Tomes, Robert, *Battles of America By Sea and Land*, vol.1 (New York: Virtue & Company, 1861).

Turnbull, J.R., 'Dazemard de Lusignan, Paul-Louis', in *Dictionary of Canadian Biography*, vol.3 (Toronto: University of Toronto/Université Laval, 2003–).

Vachon, André, 'Briand, Jean-Olivier', in *Dictionary of Canadian Biography*, vol.4 (Toronto: University of Toronto/Université Laval, 2003–).

Whiteley, William H., 'Saunders, Sir Charles', in *Dictionary of Canadian Biography*, vol.4 (Toronto: University of Toronto/Université Laval, 2003–).

Willcox, William B. (ed.), *The Papers of Benjamin Franklin*, vol.24 (New Haven, CT: Yale University Press, 1984).

Electronic Sources

Alberts, Robert C., 'Stobo, Robert', in *Dictionary of Canadian Biography*, vol.3 (Toronto: University of Toronto/Université Laval, 2003–), http://www.biographi.ca/en/bio/stobo_robert_3E.html (accessed 20 June 2019).

Anon., 'HMS *Neptune* (1757)', *Wikipedia*, www.wikipedia.com (accessed 27 August 2018).

Anon., 'Huppe/Mailhot/Royals', *Rootsweb*, https://wc.rootsweb.com/cgi-bin/igm.cgi?op=GET&db=huppe1&id=I211128 (accessed 26 July 2018).

Anon., 'Premier voyage à Saint-Domingue' https://www.decitre.fr/media/pdf/feuilletage/9/7/8/2/9/1/9/3/9782919339471.pdf (accessed 6 June 2019).

Archives Nationales D'Outre-Mer, 'Foligné Du Chalonge (François Jérôme), commander of the *Schwinton*', http://anom.archivesnationales.culture.gouv.fr/ark:/61561/bo755ztvutwm (accessed 4 September 2018).

Archives Nationales D'Outre-Mer, 'Québec. Certificats accordés à Foligné Du Chalonge (1759)', http://anom.archivesnationales.culture.gouv.fr/ark:/61561/bo755dxzzl4z (accessed 4 September 2018).

Campeau, Charles Vianney, *Navires Venus en Nouvelle-France*, http://naviresnouvellefrance.net/vaisseau1700/html/page1759.html (accessed 4 September 2018).

Carr, Thomas M. Jr., 'Writing the convent in New France: the colonialist rhetoric of Canadian nuns', *Québec Studies* 47:Spring/Summer 2009, pp.3–23, http://digitalcommons.unl.edu/modlangfrench/64.

Charland, Thomas, 'Les neveux de Madame de Beaubassin', *Revue d'Histoire de l'Amérique Française*, 23:1 (June 1969), https://www.erudit.org/en/journals/haf/1969-v23-n1-haf2070/302854ar/ (accessed 27 August 2018).

Chicago, University of, 'Dictionnaire vivant de la langue Française', ARTFL Project, https://dvlf.uchicago.edu/ (accessed 8 September 2018).

Consentino, Lucie LeBlanc, 'Hundreds perish as sea while being deported', *Acadian & French-Canadian Ancestral Home*, http://www.acadian-home.org/acadians-die-at-sea.html (accessed 1 January 2019).

Couture, Richard, '1759: British expedition against Québec – preparations and arrival', *Kronoskaf Seven Years War Project*, http://www.kronoskaf.com/syw/index.php?title=1759_-_British_expedition_against_Qu%C3%A9bec_%E2%80%93_Preparations_and_Arrival (accessed 7 June 2019).

Couture, Richard, '*Pie* (18)', *Kronoskaf Seven Years War Project*, http://www.kronoskaf.com/syw/index.php?title=Pie_(18) (accessed 7 December 2018).

Gagné, David, 'Le secteur de la Traverse', *Ville de Lévis, Service du Patrimonie et Soutien à l'Urbanisme*, (Québec: January 2013), https://www.ville.levis.qc.ca/fileadmin/Documents_PDF/Histoire-secteur-Traverse.pdf (accessed 7 December 2018).

Gaillard, Guillaume, 'La famille Gaillard de Saint-Laurent', *Le Bulletin Des Recherches*, vol.41:1935, p.14, http://collections.banq.qc.ca/jrn03/dn2087/src/1935/04/164865_1935-04.txt (accessed 11 December 2018).

Genevoy, Robert, 'Armoiries Joannès et Michel de Boucherolles au cimetière Saint Germain de Porrentruy', *Archivum Heraldicum International Bulletin*, 41:1(1967), https://www.e-periodica.ch/digbib/view?pid=ahe-002:1967:81::4#44 (accessed 13 June 2019).

Government of Canada, 'The Battle of Sainte-Foy', *The National Battlefields Commission: Plains of Abraham*, http://bataille.ccbn-nbc.gc.ca/en/bataille-de-sainte-foy/contexte/un-hiver-difficile-a-quebec.php (accessed 29 August 2018).

Government of Canada, 'Database of the 1759–1760 soldiers', *The National Battlefields Commission: Plains of Abraham*, http://www.ccbn-nbc.gc.ca/en/history-heritage/battles-1759-1760/soldiers/ (accessed 29 August 2018).

Government of Québec, 'Blaise of the Bergeres de Rigauville, Charles-Régis', *Directory of Québec's Cultural Heritage*, http://www.patrimoine-culturel.gouv.qc.ca/rpcq/detail.do?methode=consulter&id=18462&type=pge#.XBQTH2j0m00 (accessed 13 June 2019).

Graves, Donald E., 'The Anse au Foulon, 1759: Some New Theories and Some New Evidence', *The Northern Mariner* 14:4(October 2004), https://www.cnrs-scrn.org/northern_mariner/vol14/tnm_14_4_61-72.pdf (accessed 3 September 2018).

Kellow, K.N., 'Le Marquis de la Chalotais', *American War of Independence – At Sea*, http://www.awiatsea.com/conn/Le%20Marquis%20de%20la%20Chalotais%20Ship%20Beaumarchais.html (accessed 4 September 2018).

Lamole, Laurent, 'L'Ordre royale et militaire de Saint-Louis', *Les Ordres de Chevalerie*, http://lorl.free.fr/stlouis.htm (accessed 25 July 2018).

Massachusetts Historical Society, 'A Plan of Québec', *Maps of the French and Indian War*, http://www.masshist.org/maps/27Atlas16Quebec/27Atlas16Quebec.htm (accessed 30 August 2018).

Poirier, Jean, 'La toponymie de l'Île d'Orléans', *Cahiers de Géographie du Québec*, 6:12 (1962), https://www.erudit.org/fr/revues/cgq/1962-v6-n12-cgq2586/020380ar.pdf (accessed 27 August 2018), pp.183–199.

Simard, Jean, 'The Augustinian Monastery of Quebec', *Encyclopedia of French Cultural Heritage in North America* (Québec: Société Héritage de Champlain, 2008–), http://www.ameriquefrancaise.org/en/article-570/The_Augustinian_Monastery_of_Quebec.html (accessed 29 October 2018).

Toronto, University of, *Dictionary of Canadian Biography* (Toronto: University of Toronto/Université Laval, 2003–), http://www.biographi.ca/en/ (accessed September 2018).

US National Archives, Peter Timothy to Benjamin Franklin, 12 June 1777, *Founders Online*, https://founders.archives.gov/documents/Franklin/01-24-02-0122 (accessed 4 September 2018).

Wikipedia, The Free Encyclopedia, https://www.wikipedia.org/ (accessed September 2018).

Wiktionary, The Free Dictionary, https://www.wiktionary.org/ (accessed September 2018).

Index

Amherst, Maj. Gen. Jeffrey 38, 43, 93, 99
Amiot, Jean-Baptiste 81
Anse au Foulon 45, 48, 58-60
Anse de Sillery 66
Anse du Fort 75
Atalante (frigate) 29, 73-74, 87

Batiscan 74, 82, 91
Beauport 19, 25-27, 29-30, 32-34, 40, 45, 57, 60, 73, 78-80, 86, 88, 92-93, 97-99, 101-102, 111
Belle Rivière 38, 96, 109
Bernetz, *Lt. Col.* Chevalier Félicien de 31, 43, 48, 92, 101
Bienfaisant (merchantman, armed as frigate) 55, 92
Boishébert et de Raffetot, Charles Deschamps de 82
Bougainville, *Col.* Louis-Antoine, Comte de 19-20, 26, 44, 49-53, 56, 58, 60-61, 72, 87-88, 91, 93-94, 97-98, 100-103
Bourlamaque, *Col.* François-Charles de 38, 48, 96, 99, 118
Briand, Bishop Jean-Olivier 24, 65, 109-110, 114, 118, 120

Cabane des Pères 85
Cadet, Joseph-Michel 72 91
Canardière 26, 45, 56-57, 60
Cap Rouge 26-27, 36, 39, 42, 48, 56-58, 62-63, 67, 92-93, 115
Cap Santé 55, 90
Charlesbourg 19, 27, 45, 111
Chézine (merchantman armed as frigate) 19, 25
Compagnies Franches de la Marine 23
Corne, *Capt.* Chevalier de la 50
Courtemanche, Capt. Jacques-François le Gardeur de 23
Courtemanche, Lt. Augustin Legardeur de 104

Daine, François 84
Delouche de St-Denis, François 28-29, 76-77
Denoyelle de Fleurimont, *Lt.* Charles-Joseph 49
Deschambault 27, 52, 90
Detroit 38, 50
Dumas, *Capt.* Jean-Daniel 35-36, 39, 80-82, 99, 100
Duprat, *Capt.* Jean-Baptiste 34
Durell, Rear Adm. Philip 68-69

Écureuils 90, 92

Fireships 26, 28-29, 39, 74, 76-77, 82, 97-98
First Nations, people of: Abenaki 23, 34, 74, 77-78; Iroquois 77; Mic-Mac 31; Ottawa/Outaouais 77-79, 82, 85
Fort Carillon 20, 38, 48, 61, 74, 87, 96 99, 109
Fort Niagara 38, 49-50, 88, 96, 99-100
Fort St Frédéric 48, 87, 96, 99

General Hospital 18, 21-22, 26, 44-46, 60-62, 104, 106, 108
Glemet, Pierre 80, 90

Hertel, Lt. Étienne 37, 49
Hôtel Dieu 18, 51, 52, 104, 106, 109

Isle aux Coudres 21-23, 27, 32, 51, 68, 72, 74, 77
Isle aux Noix 48, 87, 96
Isle d'Orléans 21, 23-24, 27, 31-33, 40, 44, 51, 53-56, 68, 74-78, 80, 86, 93-94, 98
Isle du Bic 21, 24
Isle St Barnabé 73, 97

La Naudière, Louise-Geneviève de 37
Léry, *Capt.* Gaspard-Joseph Chaussegros de 21, 73, 77
Lévis, *Mar. de Camp.* Chevalier de 17, 20, 24, 26, 33-35, 40, 43-46, 49-50, 62, 73, 85-86, 95-97, 99, 103, 113, 119
Lignery, *Capt.* François-Marie le Marchand de 49, 96, 99
Louisbourg 34, 38, 80
Lusignan, Lt. Paul-Louis Dazemard de 89

Manon (merchantman armed as frigate) 55
Marchault (merchantman armed as frigate) 20, 55, 72
Maréchal Senneterre (merchantman armed as frigate) 55
Militia 17, 29, 34-35, 40, 56, 60-61, 71, 73, 84, 87, 97-98, 101-104, 110, 113, 118; of Montréal 26, 56
of Québec 56; of Trois Rivières 34
Miramichi 77, 82
Montcalm-Gozon, *Lt. Gén.* Louis-Joseph de 17, 20-22, 24, 26, 34-35, 40, 44, 46, 48, 50, 52-56, 59-62, 73, 85-86, 90, 96-101, 112, 113
Montmorency Falls; see Sault Montmorency
Montréal 18, 20, 24-26, 38, 48-49, 97, 104, 106, 110, 114, 117, 119
Murray, Maj. Gen. James 59, 71, 107, 115, 117

Neptune, HMS 36, 41
Niverville, Joseph-Claude Boucher de 23, 74

Ochterlony, Capt. David 46-47, 86, 91

Pays d'en Haut 73, 88
Pointe aux Trembles 40, 42, 48-49, 52-53, 55-58, 62, 82-83, 87, 91-92
Pointe de Lévy 26, 28-32, 34-36, 38, 40, 43-44, 46-48, 50-51, 55-58, 61, 63, 4-75, 77-82, 85-86, 89-94, 98-100, 110
Pontleroy, Nicolas Sarrebource de 22, 97
Pot de l'Eau de Vie 68
Pouchot, *Lt. Col.* Pierre 38, 49, 96, 99
Poulin de Courval, François-Louis 15, 92

Ramezay, Jean-Baptiste-Nicolas-Roch de 62-69, 71, 95, 101-103, 141
Récollets, order of 42, 51, 89
Regiments, French: Béarn 17, 21, 26, 34, 40, 59-60, 96; Berry 96; Guyenne 17, 21, 26, 34-35, 46, 56, 59, 99, 101; La Reine 21, 96; La Sarre 17, 26, 34-35, 40, 59-60; Languedoc 17, 21, 26, 35, 40, 59-60, 64, 91, 95; Royal Roussillon 17, 21, 26, 56, 81, 101
Repentigny, Capt. Louis Legardeur de 23-24, 34, 56, 85, 100
Rigauville, Charles-Régis Blaise Des Bergères de 116, 118
Rivière St Charles 17, 19-22, 24, 52, 63, 89, 97

St Anne 27, 33, 68, 74, 87
St Antoine 27, 49, 51, 80, 88, 90-91
St Foi 18, 27, 60, 82, 117
Saint-Sauveur, André Grasset de 47
Ste Croix 90
Sault Montmorency 20, 24-25, 32-33, 37, 54, 56, 73, 79, 82, 85, 89, 97, 99-100
Saunders, Rear. Adm. Charles 53, 66-67, 80
Senezergues de la Rodde, *Lt. Col.* Etienne-Guillaume de 17, 24
Sillery 42-45, 81, 92-95; see also Anse de Sillery
Stobo, Capt. Robert 83
Swinton (merchantman/corvette) 15

Townshend, Brig. Charles 64-66, 95
Trou de St Patrice 75, 77
Typhus 108

Ursulines, order of 36, 51-52, 62, 106, 110, 115

Vaudreuil de Cavignal, Pierre de Rigaud de 15, 17, 21, 25-26, 32, 43, 61, 63, 66, 96-99, 101-103, 106, 113
Vergor, *Capt.* Louis Dupont de Chambon de 58-59

Wolfe, Maj. Gen. James 32, 37, 40-41, 43-44, 53-54, 57, 59-61, 75, 80, 83, 85, 93, 95

From Reason to Revolution series – Warfare 1721-1815

http://www.helion.co.uk/published-by-helion/reason-to-revolution-1721-1815.html

The 'From Reason to Revolution' series covers the period of military history 1721–1815, an era in which fortress-based strategy and linear battles gave way to the nation-in-arms and the beginnings of total war.

This era saw the evolution and growth of light troops of all arms, and of increasingly flexible command systems to cope with the growing armies fielded by nations able to mobilise far greater proportions of their manpower than ever before. Many of these developments were fired by the great political upheavals of the era, with revolutions in America and France bringing about social change which in turn fed back into the military sphere as whole nations readied themselves for war. Only in the closing years of the period, as the reactionary powers began to regain the upper hand, did a military synthesis of the best of the old and the new become possible.

The series will examine the military and naval history of the period in a greater degree of detail than has hitherto been attempted, and has a very wide brief, with the intention of covering all aspects from the battles, campaigns, logistics, and tactics, to the personalities, armies, uniforms, and equipment.

Submissions

The publishers would be pleased to receive submissions for this series. Please contact series editor Andrew Bamford via email (andrewbamford18@gmail.com), or in writing to Helion & Company Limited, Unit 8 Amherst Business Centre, Budbrooke Road, Warwick, CV34 5WE

Titles

No 1 *Lobositz to Leuthen. Horace St Paul and the Campaigns of the Austrian Army in the Seven Years War 1756-57* Translated with additional materials by Neil Cogswell (ISBN 978-1-911096-67-2)

No 2 *Glories to Useless Heroism. The Seven Years War in North America from the French journals of Comte Maurés de Malartic, 1755-1760* William Raffle (ISBN 978-1-1911512-19-6) (paperback)

No 3 *Reminiscences 1808-1815 Under Wellington. The Peninsular and Waterloo Memoirs of William Hay* William Hay, with notes and commentary by Andrew Bamford (ISBN 978-1-1911512-32-5)

No 4 *Far Distant Ships. The Royal Navy and the Blockade of Brest 1793-1815* Quintin Barry (ISBN 978-1-1911512-14-1)

No 5 *Godoy's Army. Spanish Regiments and Uniforms from the Estado Militar of 1800* Charles Esdaile and Alan Perry (ISBN 978-1-911512-65-3) (paperback)

No 6 *On Gladsmuir Shall the Battle Be! The Battle of Prestonpans 1745* Arran Johnston (ISBN 978-1-911512-83-7)

No 7 *The French Army of the Orient 1798-1801. Napoleon's Beloved 'Egyptians'* Yves Martin (ISBN 978-1-911512-71-4)*

No 8 *The Autobiography, or Narrative of a Soldier. The Peninsular War Memoirs of William Brown of the 45th Foot* William Brown, with notes and commentary by Steve Brown (ISBN 978-1-911512-94-3) (paperback)

No 9 *Recollections from the Ranks. Three Russian Soldiers' Autobiographies from the Napoleonic Wars* Translated and annotated by Darrin Boland (ISBN 978-1-912174-18-8) (paperback)

No 10 *By Fire and Bayonet. Grey's West Indies Campaign of 1794* Steve Brown (ISBN 978-1-911512-60-8)

No 11 *Olmütz to Torgau. Horace St Paul and the Campaigns of the Austrian Army in the Seven Years War 1758-60* Translated with additional materials by Neil Cogswell (ISBN 978-1-911512-72-1)

No 12 *Murat's Army. The Army of the Kingdom of Naples 1806-1815* Digby Smith (ISBN 978-1-912390-09-0) (paperback)

No 13 *The Veteran or 40 Years' Service in the British Army. The Scurrilous Recollections of Paymaster John Harley 47th Foot – 1798-1838* John Harley, with notes and commentary by Gareth Glover (ISBN 978-1-912390-25-0) (paperback)

No 14 *Narrative of the Eventful Life of Thomas Jackson. Militiaman and Coldstream Sergeant, 1803-15* Thomas Jackson, with notes and commentary by Eamonn O'Keeffe (ISBN 978-1-912390-12-0) (paperback)

No 15 *For Orange and the States! The Army of the Dutch Republic 1713-1772. Part I: Infantry* Marc Geerdinck-Schaftenaar (ISBN 978-1-911512-15-8)*

No 16 *'Men who are Determined to be Free': The American Assault on Stony Point 15 July 1779* David Bonk (ISBN 978-1-912174-84-3)*

No 17 *Next to Wellington. General Sir George Murray. The Story of a Scottish Soldier and Statesman, Wellington's Quartermaster General* John Harding-Edgar (ISBN 978-1-912390-13-7)

No 18 *Between Scylla and Charybdis: The Army of Friedrich August II of Saxony, 1733-1763. Part I: Staff and Cavalry* Marco Pagan (ISBN 978-1-912174-89-8)*

No 19 *The Secret Expedition: The Anglo-Russian Invasion of Holland 1799* Geert van Uythoven (ISBN 978-1-912390-20-5)

No 20 *'We Are Accustomed to do our Duty' German Auxiliaries with the British Army 1793-95* Paul Demet (ISBN 978-1-912174-96-6)

No 21 *With the Guards in Flanders. The Diary of Captain Roger Morris 1793-95* Peter Harington (ISBN 978-1-911628-15-6) (paperback)

No 22 *The British Army in Egypt 1801. An Underrated Army Comes of Age* Carole Divall (ISBN 978-1-911628-17-0)*

No 23 *Better is the Proud Plaid. The Clothing, Weapons, and Accoutrements of the Jacobites in 1745* Jenn Scott (ISBN ISBN 978-1-911628-16-3)*

No 24 *The Lilies and the Thistle. French Troops in the Jacobite '45* Andrew Bamford (ISBN 978-1-911628-17-0)*

No 25 *A Light Infantryman With Wellington* Gareth Glover (ed.) (ISBN 978-1-911628-10-1) (paperback)

No 26 *Swiss Regiments in the Service of France 1798-1815. Uniforms, Organisation, Campaigns* Stephen Ede-Borrett (ISBN 978-1-911628-12-5)*

No 27 *For Orange and the States! The Army of the Dutch Republic 1713-1772. Part II: Cavalry and Specialist Troops* Marc Geerdinck-Schaftenaar (ISBN 978-1-911628-13-2)*

No 28 *Fashioning Regulation, Regulating Fashion. Uniforms and Dress of the British Army 1800-1815 Volume I* Ben Townsend (ISBN 978-1-911628-09-5)

No 29 *Riflemen. The History of the 5th Battalion 60th (Royal American) Regiment, 1797-1818* Robert Griffith (ISBN 978-1-911628-46-0)

No 30 *The Key to Lisbon. The Third French Invasion of Portugal, 1810-11* Kenton White (ISBN 978-1-911628-52-1)

No 31 *Command and Leadership. Proceedings of the 2018 Helion & Company 'From Reason to Revolution' Conference* Andrew Bamford (ed.) (ISBN 978-1-911628-53-8)

No 32 *Waterloo After the Glory. Hospital Sketches and Reports on the Wounded After the Battle* Michael Crumplin and Gareth Glover (ISBN 978-1-911628-48-4)

No 33 *Fluxes, Fevers, and Fighting Men. War and Disease in Ancien Regime Europe 1648-1789* Pádraig Lenihan (ISBN 978-1-911628-51-4)

No 34 *'They Were Good Soldiers'. African-Americans Serving in the Continental Army, 1775-1783* John U. Rees (ISBN 978-1-911628-54-5)*

No 35 *A Redcoat in America. The Diaries of Lieutenant William Bamford, 1757-1765 and 1776* Edited and Annotated by John B. Hattendorf (ISBN 978-1-911628-47-7) (paperback)

No 36 *Between Scylla and Charybdis: The Army of Friedrich August II of Saxony, 1733-1763. Part II: Infantry and Artillery* Marco Pagan (ISBN 978-1-911628-08-8)*

No 37 *Québec Under Siege: French Eye-Witness Accounts from the Campaign of 1759* Translated and Annotated by Charles A. Mayhood (ISBN 978-1-912866-73-1) (paperback)

* indicates 'Falconet' format paperbacks, page size 248mm x 180 mm, with high visual content including colour plates; other titles are hardback monographs unless otherwise noted.